How Emmerson Mnangagwa Blindsided Robert Mugabe
and Grabbed Zimbabwe

HOW EMMERSON MNANGAGWA BLINDSIDED ROBERT MUGABE AND GRABBED ZIMBABWE

THE GENESIS

AN AUTOBIOGRAPHY BY
LOVEMORE ITAI MUKANDI

LOVEMORE ITAI MUKANDI

lovemoremukandi@gmail.com

TABLE OF CONTENTS

DEDICATION

I dedicate this book to my wife and soul-mate Sibongile, who has stood by me through all days, months and years, whether 'diamond or stone', and without whose enduring support and love I would not have achieved much.

I also dedicate the book to my daughters Lisa, Kundisai, Tamara, and Tanaka, as well as my son Bryan and my sister-in-law Rufaro.

Last, but by no means least, I dedicate this book to the resilient people of Zimbabwe.

PREFACE

THIS BOOK IS a first-hand account of some of the events and processes which shaped the destiny of Zimbabwe during the era of President Robert Gabriel Mugabe, leading up to his eventual overthrow by Emmerson Dambudzo Mnangagwa, assisted by the army in a military coup, in November 2017. Mugabe was Prime Minister of Zimbabwe from independence on 18th April 1980 until 1987, when he became President following a constitutional amendment. He was the President of Zimbabwe until his overthrow. The coup in November 2017 was led by the Commander of the Zimbabwe Defense Forces General Constantine Chiwenga, who was appointed Vice-President of Zimbabwe by Mnangagwa after he became President of Zimbabwe following the coup. Before the 2017 coup, Emmerson Mnangagwa had served in various ministerial portfolios under Mugabe since Zimbabwe's independence. He had served as Minister of State for National Security, Minister of Justice, Minister of Defense and Speaker of Parliament, among other portfolios. He had even been Mugabe's Personal and Special Assistant during Zimbabwe's liberation war in the late 1970s, and so he was very close to Mugabe and was widely regarded as Mugabe's right-hand man.

While he was Minister of State for National Security, during the years 1980-1988, Mnangagwa was head of the Central Intelligence Organization (the CIO). As an intelligence organization, the

CIO ought to have been apolitical, but Mnangagwa had transformed it into a formidable tool to intimidate or even eliminate political opponents, and to promote his own personal political ambitions.

The book's main thrust is to trace the roots and origins of the Mnangagwa regime to events which took place during the Mugabe era. It shows how certain persons in key positions in Mugabe's government, led by Mnangagwa, deliberately aided the efforts by Mnangagwa to assume power without Mugabe realizing it. It also shows how other key persons in Mugabe's government were indifferent to what was going on, even though they knew or at least suspected what Mnangagwa was up to and had the opportunity to stop him, but either gave Mnangagwa the benefit of the doubt or decided to sit on the fence because of their high risk-aversion; by so doing they were complicit in the actions by Mnangagwa that eventually led to Mugabe's overthrow. It is important to observe that while the Mugabe regime was brutal and was associated with widespread human rights violations, the post-coup Mnangagwa government has become associated with even more brutality and autocratic tendencies. Millions of Zimbabweans went out onto the streets throughout Zimbabwe to celebrate Mugabe's overthrow in November 2017, but in just seven years since then there is now deep nostalgia for the Mugabe era by most Zimbabweans, who now feel they enjoyed relatively more liberty and economic prosperity under the Mugabe government than they do now under the Mnangagwa government.

This book traces the origins of the Mnangagwa regime to plots and deception by Mnangagwa against Mugabe during the latter's era. The main point to note is that there is anecdotal evidence that Mnangagwa had, as far back as the 1980s, set his sights on taking over power from Mugabe, and was determined to achieve that objective by capturing the State apparatus from Mugabe while professing to be loyal to him. Mnangagwa recruited key officials in all arms of the State, particularly in the judiciary, the Office of the President and Cabinet, the military and the CIO, to be loyal to him and disloyal to Mugabe, with the clear objective of blindsiding Mugabe and taking over power from him. This network of influential people, which included members of the business community, bankers and lawyers, was bound together mostly by a common tribal connection with Mnangagwa. Unbeknown to Mugabe, who displayed misplaced and absolute trust in Mnangagwa much of the time, many key officials reported sensitive State matters not to Mugabe but to Mnangagwa. Mnangagwa knew that he lacked charisma and could not win elections at the ruling party congress for leadership; neither could he win free and fair national presidential elections. By capturing the State apparatus and recruiting this network, Mnangagwa had started preparations to assume power through undemocratic means as far back as the 1980s, and this process culminated in the November 2017 military coup.

The book is written in the form of an autobiography by the author, who holds the following university degrees: Bachelor of Law (B.L.) and Bachelor of Laws (LLB) from the University of Zimbabwe; Bachelor of Arts (Hons.)

Economics, Bachelor of Commerce major in Finance, and Master of Arts in Economics from universities in Canada. The author was also a doctoral (PhD) candidate in Economics at the University of Cape Town (U.C.T.) in South Africa, at the time of writing this book.

The book provides an autobiography of the author in some depth, to give the reader an appreciation of how access to this account was obtained. The autobiography covers the author's early life, educational background, an account of the brief period the author spent in Mozambique during Zimbabwe's liberation war (1978-1980), and an account of the eighteen years (1980-1998) spent working for the CIO, Zimbabwe's spy agency. This latter period covers service as a diplomat in Mozambique and Romania, as a legal advisor to the Minister of State for National Security in the President's Office, as a Director of Administration in the CIO and, ultimately, as second in command of the CIO, in the position of Deputy Director General. The autobiography ends with a description of the events leading to the author going into exile in Canada in the year 2001, and to his deportation from Canada in the year 2011. It also briefly covers the five years spent in Cape Town, South Africa, as a doctoral (PhD) student in Economics at the University of Cape Town (2015-2019).

An extensive account is given to encounters that the author had, directly or indirectly, with Mnangagwa while he was Minister of State for National Security in the President's Office, then later Minister of Justice, and later still Speaker of the National Assembly. In particular, Mnangagwa served on the Committee of Ministers appointed by President Mugabe to mediate in the armed conflict between the Mozambican government and the Mozambican armed resistance (RENAMO), while the author served on the Committee of Officials appointed to assist the Committee of Ministers. There were numerous encounters the author had with Mnangagwa within Zimbabwe and in countries like Mozambique, Malawi, Kenya, Italy and the United Kingdom, where meetings took place in connection with the Mozambican mediation process.

As a result of several years of working together, during the period 1989-1998, Mnangagwa has personal knowledge of the author and the author has fairly deep knowledge of Mnangagwa, and this comes across from the account which follows in the autobiography.

In addition to interactions with Mnangagwa, the author also had numerous interactions with President Mugabe himself, and with Dr. Sydney Sekeramayi, who was the Minister of State for National Security in the President's Office, after Mnangagwa was moved from that portfolio and appointed Minister of Justice in the year 1988. There was day-to-day interaction between the author and Dr. Elleck Mashingaidze, who was the CIO Director General during the period 1992-1997. There were also numerous interactions between the author and military and police commanders, such as former police commissioners Henry Mukurazhizha and Augustine Chihuri, General Solomon Mujuru, General Vitalis Zvinavashe, General Constantine Chiwenga, Air Chief Marshall Josiah Tungamirai and

Air Chief Marshall Perence Shiri. Mujuru, Zvinavashe, Tungamirai, and Shiri are now deceased.

The book also observes that following the November 2017 military coup Mnangagwa, apart from appointing General Chiwenga Vice-President, also appointed Air Chief Marshall Perence Shiri, who had been Commander of the Airforce of Zimbabwe, to a cabinet position as Minister of Lands and Agriculture. This indicates that both General Chiwenga and Air Chief Marshall Perence Shiri were actively involved in the coup. The book investigates what brought Mnangagwa, General Chiwenga and Air Chief Marshall Shiri together in this plot, and finds that there were credible press reports indicating that General Chiwenga and Air Chief Marshall Shiri worked closely with Mnangagwa during the Gukurahundi military operations in Matabeleland, in western Zimbabwe, in the 1980s. The operations resulted in atrocities involving the massacre of up to 20,000 civilians by the Fifth Brigade and other units of the Zimbabwe Defense and Security Forces, and there was an international outcry against the operation and demands for accountability by human rights groups. The common fear of facing justice one day, to account for those atrocities, is what the author believes brought together Mnangagwa, Air Chief Marshall Perence Shiri and General Chiwenga. They were all actively involved in and led the brutal and fatal operations against civilians and political opposition in the post-independence history of Zimbabwe. The author believes that fear was also a strong motivation for the timing of the

November 2017 military coup, to ensure that anyone they did not trust to protect them once in power was prevented from assuming power. The coup plotters realized in the year 2017 that President Mugabe was about to hand over power because of advanced age and deteriorating health, and that fear made them pre-empt a transfer of power by President Mugabe to someone who they feared would not protect them in the future from prosecution, for crimes against humanity and genocide committed against civilians in Matabeleland in the 1980s.

Shiri died from what was publicly described as Covid-19 complications, in the year 2020.

The author also describes the events surrounding the shooting of Patrick Kombayi during the 1990 parliamentary election campaigns in Gweru, and the prosecution of Elias Kanengoni and Kizito Chivamba in connection with the shooting. Kombayi was a businessman, former Mayor of Gweru, and organizing secretary of the short-lived opposition Zimbabwe Unity Movement political party, and was contesting the Gweru urban seat against Vice- President Simon Muzenda. Kanengoni was the head of the CIO Midlands Provincial Office, while Chivamba was a senior official of the ruling party ZANU (P.F.). Kanengoni and Chivamba were both charged with and convicted of the attempted murder of Kombayi, and were subsequently pardoned by President Mugabe. The author sheds more light on the circumstances surrounding this episode, and describes the political intrigue associated with the prosecution of Kanengoni and Chivamba. This was a deliberately misdirected prosecution which saved the real culprit from prosecution, because his prosecution would have implicated Vice-President Muzenda. The involvement of Mnangagwa, who was Minister of Justice at the time, and Patrick Chinamasa, who was Attorney General, and whose office was responsible for criminal prosecutions at the time of the intrigue, is discussed in this autobiography.

In Part Two of the autobiography, the author also shows the close working relationship which existed over the years between Mnangagwa and Eddison Shirihuru, who was Deputy Director General of the CIO until his death in August 1993. Shirihuru was at the time of his death accused of the disappearance of Rashiwe Guzha, a typist with the Treasury Computer Bureau, who was believed to have had a romantic relationship with Shirihuru immediately prior to her disappearance. The police never got to establish what happened to her.

There is a description in Part Two of the autobiography of President Mugabe's disciplinarian disposition. He displayed a very serious attitude most of the time and rarely smiled in public. He at one time told a meeting attended by the author that he required people attending his meetings to sit upright in chairs and not to relax in couches, which were meant for people who wanted to take a nap. In another episode, President Mugabe banned Shirihuru from accompanying him on his foreign visits for months, after Shirihuru had staggered into President Mugabe's hotel suite in a drunken stupor during one of the President's foreign visits.

The autobiography also describes an encounter the author had with the late General Solomon Mujuru, to discuss the threat posed by Mnangagwa to Mugabe's presidency. Solomon Mujuru was a highly decorated General, and was deputy to General Josiah Magama Tongogara in the ZANLA (Zimbabwe African National Liberation Army) hierarchy during Zimbabwe's liberation war. He was Commander of the Zimbabwe National Army after Zimbabwe's independence in 1980. That informal meeting – which the author had with the General during a drive from the General's offices in Milton Park to Kuwadzana in Harare and back – was arranged for the author by the General's wife Mrs. Joyce Mujuru, while she was still a cabinet minister in the year 1998. The author believes that had the General taken his advice seriously, perhaps the destiny of Zimbabwe could have turned out differently, and the General's death thirteen years later could have been averted; he was burnt to death in a fire in very suspicious circumstances, in his house in Beatrice, forty kilometres south of Harare, in August 2011.

General Mujuru had, after the informal meeting with the author, and to the author's great disappointment, influenced Dr. Sekeramayi – who was Minister of State for National Security in the President's Office – and President Mugabe to remove the author and Shadreck Chipanga from their positions as Deputy Director General and Director General respectively, and to replace them by two brigadiers from the Zimbabwe National Army, who were friends of the General, in the mistaken belief that the General would wrestle control over the CIO away from Mnangagwa that way, and be in control of the organization through them. Chipanga had been staunchly pro-Mnangagwa, and I was seen by the Mnangagwa camp as pro-Mujuru. The General thought the removal of Chipanga and I from the leadership of the CIO simultaneously would be regarded by the Mnangagwa camp as fair. Our replacement by the two brigadiers was considered by the General as a subtle victory for him, because few knew that they were in fact Mujuru's loyalists.

One of the brigadiers, Happyton Bonyongwe, later became CIO Director General. However, people like Isaac Moyo, who were close to Mnangagwa, would be recommended for promotion by Bonyongwe and seconded to the Ministry of Foreign Affairs to become Ambassador to South Africa. The error of judgment in so doing, on the part of Bonyongwe and General Mujuru, if they believed they had taken control over the CIO away from Mnangagwa, is demonstrated by the fact that Isaac Moyo was appointed CIO Director General by Mnangagwa, soon after overthrowing President Mugabe in November 2017. In other words, did Mujuru accomplish his objective of wrestling control of the CIO away from Mnangagwa, by having the two brigadiers assume the top leadership of the CIO, or were the brigadiers neutralized and made to switch loyalties once they assumed their new positions in the CIO?

The author shows how, during his service in the CIO, he came to be regarded by some senior officers who were loyal to Mnangagwa as belonging to a political faction associated with General Mujuru, which was challenging and resisting Mnangagwa's political ambitions. When Chipanga, a pro-Mnangagwa officer, was head of the CIO, the author became the victim of public mudslinging, which culminated in politically motivated criminal charges being made against him. The author was arrested and continued to be pursued by the police, who were being pushed by the CIO to do so even after he was removed from remand by a court, forcing the author to go into exile in Canada. The pro-Mnangagwa CIO and police officers were so determined to victimize the author that they made the false claim to a magistrate that the author had absconded from Zimbabwe and obtained a warrant of arrest against him, which they used to ask Interpol to seek the author's deportation from Canada and enforced return to Zimbabwe. The author was deported from Canada in 2011 and arrested on arrival in Zimbabwe, but a magistrate freed him after realizing that the warrant of arrest used to bring the author back from Canada had been fraudulently obtained by the police. They and the CIO had conspired with a magistrate to issue a warrant of arrest, which falsely claimed that the author was a fugitive from justice, yet he had left Zimbabwe lawfully, after being removed from remand by a competent court.

The autobiography which follows is in three parts. Part One covers the early life and educational background of the author, as well as the period of his participation in the liberation war of Zimbabwe. Part Two covers the period of the author's service in the CIO, and is the central part of the autobiography. The last part, Part Three, covers the author's post-CIO service period.

PART
ONE

EARLY LIFE, EDUCATIONAL BACKGROUND AND PARTICIPATION IN ZIMBABWE'S LIBERATION WAR

I WAS BORN on 15th April 1957, in Chikomba District in Zimbabwe, and grew up on a family-owned farm in the Mutoro small-scale farming area, about forty kilometres north-east of Chivhu. Chivhu is a small town, located in an agricultural area about one hundred and forty kilometres south of Zimbabwe's capital, Harare. I am the eldest in a family of seven, comprising four girls and three boys. During school holidays, life was all about tilling the maize and groundnut fields and looking after the small herd of cattle on the farm.

I attended Kwenda Mission, a Methodist school east of Chivhu, and took part in church choirs, but did very little else apart from working hard to pass my Cambridge Ordinary Level studies. In the year 1975 I went to Hartzell High School, a United Methodist school near Mutare in eastern Zimbabwe, for my Cambridge Advanced Level studies, where I took English, History and Geography, which I passed well enough to be admitted to the University of Rhodesia (as the University of Zimbabwe was then known) in 1977.

I studied Law at the university and, having passed my first year, I proceeded into the second year in 1978. The country was still under colonialism and was known as Rhodesia at the time. By 1978, the political situation in the country had become tense, with the liberation war spreading rapidly across the country from neighbouring Mozambique and Zambia.

I had first become acutely aware of the revolutionary atmosphere gripping the country during my years in high school at Hartzell, in 1975 and 1976. Being close to the border with Mozambique, from where fighters belonging to the Zimbabwe African National Liberation Army (ZANLA) were infiltrating the country, the general atmosphere at Hartzell High School was revolutionary and some of the teachers who taught me – in particular the history teacher – spent a lot of time discussing in class the state of the liberation war and its political objectives. The atmosphere became even more heated with the death of the ZANU (Zimbabwe African National Union) chairman Herbert Chitepo, in Zambia in 1975, a death which was widely suspected to have been the result of a political assassination. During the same year, while I was at Hartzell High School, Robert Mugabe – who was to become the Prime Minister of Zimbabwe at independence in 1980 – and Edgar Tekere – who was ZANU (PF) Secretary General at independence – crossed the border into Mozambique, and the momentum of the liberation war in Zimbabwe intensified.

It was against that background – and also because of the decision in 1978 by the Rhodesian government to conscript adult males of all races into the Rhodesian army – that I and a few fellow university students decided to join the liberation war. Accordingly, I abandoned my law studies in the year 1978 and went to Mozambique in the company of five fellow university students. We took a bus from Harare to Mutare and proceeded to Hartzell High

School, where my previous history teacher drove us and dropped us off at Manica Bridge, north of Mutare. There, war collaborators who ran errands for liberation fighters promptly escorted us to meet ZANLA fighters, who were conducting military operations in the area.

The living conditions in Mozambique, when I crossed the border with my fellow university students in 1978, were very difficult. Food was scarce and sometimes consisted of just boiled maize grains. It did not help matters that some trained fighters were suspicious of our motive in joining the liberation war, and thought we may have been spies sent by the Rhodesian government to report on their activities. They had difficulty understanding how people living comfortably at the university could give all that up and join the liberation war, with all its known associated hardships. It rained a lot in the central Mozambican province of Manica, where we were based, and there was no shelter. Our clothes quickly got torn and there were no clothes to replace them.

We were soon split up and I never got to know the fate of some of my fellow university students. I was sent to Tete Province in Mozambique, to a training camp named Tembwe. The place was extremely hot and food was scarce. It rained a lot there and floods were common, making the delivery of food replenishments impossible at times. In spite of the hardships, military training soon started and it was very gruelling. It lasted almost three months, and I was relieved to be selected to be part of a group that was sent to Maputo, the Mozambican capital, en route to

Romania for a combined intelligence and military training course, which was to last another three months.

It was a big relief to be in Romania, as that meant having access to food, shelter and relative comfort. It was winter in Romania when we arrived, in January 1979, but we had warm clothing.

On completing the training in Romania, we were flown back to Mozambique and deployed to a military base in Mavhonde, in Manica Province. Since I had been trained in intelligence in Romania, I was attached to a security and intelligence unit at the base, with responsibilities which included interviewing new recruits, in an effort to detect any spies among them.

The security portfolio in the bases in Mozambique during the war was led by the late General Vitalis Zvinavashe, known then as Commander Gava. Among his colleagues in the top ranks in ZANLA, he was fondly known as "Fox", a literal English translation of the Shona word "Gava". He was in the camps most of the time, but periodically went to Maputo to report to his boss, Emmerson Mnangagwa, who was based in Maputo and was Special Assistant to the President of ZANU (P.F.), Robert Mugabe. Thus, Mnangagwa was already working in close proximity to Mugabe.

A major attack of the Mavhonde base by the Rhodesian army took place around September 1979, during the time of the Lancaster House Conference – a conference which ended with the signing of a ceasefire agreement and brought to an end the Zimbabwe liberation war. I was in the base and survived the attack.

When the ceasefire was signed, I was selected by Commander Gava to go to Maputo, where I was in early 1980 selected to be part of a group of trained fighters to escort a convoy of Toyota Landcruiser vehicles, which were driven from Maputo to Harare via Mutare, to be part of a fleet of vehicles to be used for election campaigns in 1980 by ZANU (P.F.). The vehicles were, however, impounded by the Rhodesian government at the border near Mutare, in an effort by the government to cripple the ZANU (P.F.) campaign machinery and adversely influence the election outcome against ZANU (P.F.). We spent nearly a month in Mutare awaiting the release of the vehicles, before finally heading to Harare, where the vehicles were distributed to top-ranking ZANU (P.F.) officials just before the 1980 general election, which ZANU (P.F.) won, paving the way to Zimbabwe's independence on 18th April 1980.

IN LATER YEARS, I was to be allowed by Emmerson Mnangagwa to complete my law studies while on study leave after independence, while working for the Central Intelligence Organization (CIO), which he headed as Minister of State for National Security in the President's Office, during the period 1980 to 1988. In that regard, I went back to the University of Zimbabwe in 1984 and graduated with a Bachelor of Law (B.L.) in 1985 and a Bachelor of Laws (LLB) degree in 1986, and was awarded a Butterworth Book Prize for being the best LLB student of the year. In addition, as described in Part Three of this autobiography, in later years I obtained Bachelor of Arts (Hons.) in Economics and Bachelor of Commerce major in Finance *(magna cum laude)* degrees from Saint Mary's University in Halifax, Canada, as well as a Master of Arts degree in Economics from Carleton University in Ottawa, Canada. I got inducted into the Hall of Fame of the President of Saint Mary's University in 2005, for my excellent academic accomplishment at the university. At the time of writing this autobiography, in February/March 2020, I had completed the required coursework for a PhD degree in Economics at the University of Cape Town in South Africa, and had handed in the final draft of my PhD dissertation to my academic supervisor, Professor Haim Abraham, as the first stage in the process of having the dissertation assessed by examiners.

PART
TWO

MY SERVICE IN THE CENTRAL
INTELLIGENCE ORGANIZATION (CIO)

I FIRST MET Emmerson Mnangagwa in the year 1980, following my appointment as First Secretary to the Embassy of Zimbabwe in Mozambique. A small group of about ten officers that I was part of had been appointed by the CIO as diplomats, and Mnangagwa, as Minister of State for National Security in the then Prime Minister's Office and head of the CIO, addressed us and explained that we were going to be declared intelligence officers serving in Zimbabwe embassies, meaning that we would be known to host intelligence services as intelligence officers, and that we would be liaising with them while performing other diplomatic duties in the embassies. Other members of the group included Nicholas Goche, who was posted to Washington, Christopher Mutsvangwa, who was posted to Brussels, Henry Maturure, who was posted to Addis Ababa and Kufa Chinoza, who was posted to London. Goche was to become a minister in Mugabe's cabinet in later years, and Mutsvangwa was to become a close advisor to Mnangagwa, following the November 2017 coup which deposed Mugabe. My career in the CIO had begun.

I served in Mozambique from 1980 to 1982. During that period I saw Mnangagwa only once, when he visited Mozambique on official duty, and I started to get to know him. In 1982 I was transferred to Romania and served in the Zimbabwe Embassy in Bucharest, the Romanian capital, during the rule of Nicolae Ceausescu, the late Romanian dictator.

I served in the embassy in Romania until the end of 1983, when I was recalled to Harare, then spent the next three years in full-time study, on study leave granted to me by Mnangagwa, completing my law studies at the University of Zimbabwe. After graduating with Bachelor of Law (B.L.) and Bachelor of Laws (LLB) degrees in 1985 and 1986 respectively, I went back to work at CIO headquarters in Harare.

I did not meet Mnangagwa again until after he had ceased to be the head of the CIO. Mnangagwa, as Minister of State for National Security in the President's Office (Prime Minister's Office until 1987), was based on the fourth floor of Chaminuka Building in Harare, the CIO headquarters. He occupied an entire wing on the fourth floor, which he shared with two secretaries, as well as his legal advisor and the legal advisor's secretary. The legal advisor to Mnangagwa was John Ngara, and Ngara's secretary was Auxillia, who was later to become Auxillia Mnangagwa, after marrying Mnangagwa. I am confident that their courtship started while Auxillia was secretary to John Ngara, even though Mnangagwa was a married man at the time. Mnangagwa and Auxillia worked in very close proximity on that fourth-floor wing, which was occupied by just them and the minister's two secretaries, as well as John Ngara.

In early 1988, two events occurred which were to dramatically impact my career in the CIO. Firstly, President Mugabe announced a cabinet reshuffle in which he moved Mnangagwa from the portfolio of Minister of State for National Security in the President's Office to that of Minister of Justice, Legal and Parliamentary Affairs.

Mnangagwa had been Minister of State for National Security since independence in 1980, and in that portfolio he had been head of the CIO. In the 1988 cabinet reshuffle, President Mugabe replaced Mnangagwa with Dr. Sydney Sekeramayi, as Minister of State for National Security in the President's Office.

The second event was that two months after the cabinet reshuffle, in March 1988, John Ngara was involved in a fatal car crash near Norton, about forty kilometres west of Harare. There was a lot of speculation at the time in the CIO about the cause of the car crash. John Ngara and Mnangagwa were regarded by many as having been very close on a personal level; they were believed to have been acquaintances from the years Mnangagwa lived in Zambia, before he went to Mozambique to join the liberation war. Ngara and a number of other senior CIO officers, who had lived in Zambia at the same time as Mnangagwa, were said to have been brought by him into the CIO, when Mnangagwa became Minister of State for National Security at or after independence in 1980. Ngara was believed to have been traumatized by Mnangagwa's departure from the CIO, as a result of the cabinet reshuffle in 1988, and this was suspected to have led him to lose focus even while driving, resulting in the car crash.

John Ngara had been Mnangagwa's close confidante, and had been assigned by Mnangagwa very sensitive tasks. Ngara had, for example, sat on the four-man Chihambakwe Commission, which had been appointed by Mugabe in 1983, to examine and report on the events which had led to the killing of thousands of civilians in Matabeleland, during the early years of Zimbabwe's independence by Zimbabwe's security forces. The Commission was headed by Simplisius Chihambakwe, a prominent lawyer, and included Ngara, Prince Machaya, who is a former Attorney General, and a member of the Zimbabwe National Army. The report of the Commission was never published and Mnangagwa was probably its custodian, since he directed the operations which went on in Matabeleland during the time of the disturbances in the 1980s. I never had sight of the report and I am not aware if Dr. Sekeramayi ever did, either.

A month or two after John Ngara's death, I was appointed to replace him as legal advisor, and so by April 1988 I had become legal advisor to Dr. Sydney Sekeramayi, the new Minister of State for National Security in the President's Office. I was not just legal advisor but I was also a special assistant to Dr Sekeramayi, just as Ngara had been to Mnangagwa. In that position I advised Minister Sekeramayi on all legal matters affecting the CIO, and I liaised with other security ministries such as the Ministry of Home Affairs and the Ministry of Defense. I worked closely with the Ministry of Justice, which is the formal legal advisor to government through the Attorney General's Office. Close consultation and liaison with the Ministry of Justice was therefore essential in my role as legal advisor to the Minister of State for National Security in the President's Office. Since Mnangagwa was now the Minister of Justice, directly or indirectly, I was to interact with him often in my new role as legal advisor in the CIO.

As special assistant to the Minister of State for National Security I had the responsibility to advise the minister on administrative and political matters affecting his portfolio and the CIO. Members of the CIO are strictly not civil servants and are not regulated by the Public Service Commission; requirements of secrecy require that the

CIO has its own administrative machinery, which is less visible to the public. Thus, while the CIO uses the Public Service Regulations as a guideline for administrative purposes, the Minister of State for National Security in the President's Office and the CIO Director General are the ultimate authority in administrative matters in the CIO, and CIO disciplinary boards which inquire into the wrongdoing and punishment of CIO offenders are approved by the Director General and the Minister. I had the responsibility to advise the Minister on the legality and fairness or otherwise of these disciplinary proceedings.

I was legal advisor to the Minister of State for National Security at a time when Zimbabwe was under a state of emergency, which had been introduced in 1965 by the Rhodesian government. Under the state of emergency detentions of political prisoners without trial were common. I realized that some senior CIO officers found it convenient to operate under a state of emergency, as it gave the CIO and the police powers to detain suspects without trial, and to hold them in detention for extended periods of time. It was apparent that, during the time Mnangagwa headed the CIO, there had been no attempts to review the need for these emergency regulations, nor to examine the associated human rights implications.

I sat down with Dr. Sekeramayi and we agreed that there had to be a paradigm shift in the way the CIO conducted its operations. There was evidence that people were being detained for extended periods of time without trial by the CIO and the police, in clear abuse of the emergency regulations. Without the regulations, the CIO had no powers of arrest, and it was desirable to remove from the CIO powers of arrest, as that would reduce the incidence of human rights violations. It was against that background that consultations were held with the Ministry of Home Affairs, leading to a broad consensus on the impropriety of the continuation of the state of emergency. After the matter had been debated in the Cabinet Committee on Legislation and in Cabinet, the government finally recommended to parliament the lifting of the state of emergency. Consequently, the state of emergency was lifted in Zimbabwe in July 1990.

I must point out that this new, less repressive style of leadership of the CIO led to widespread resentment against Dr. Sekeramayi among some senior CIO officers, and a nostalgia for Mnangagwa's time in the CIO. Dr. Sekeramayi was described as "weak" and "indecisive" in comparison with Mnangagwa, by some senior CIO officers who remained close to Mnangagwa after his departure from the CIO.

While there was widespread longing for Mnangagwa among some middle and top CIO ranks, there was palpable resentment against him among lower ranks in the organization. It was alleged by lower-level officers that Mnangagwa surrounded himself mostly with people from his tribe and home region of Masvingo/Midlands, as well as those who had lived with him in Zambia, or were former political detainees like him. Widespread irregularities in CIO disciplinary proceedings were alleged to have occurred during Mnangagwa's time in the CIO, resulting in outright persecution of CIO members who did not belong to Mnangagwa's tribe or who had not lived in Zambia with him. Thus, in the aftermath of the 1988 cabinet reshuffle, there were those in the CIO who had harsh words for President Mugabe for causing Mnangagwa's departure from the CIO, and a majority of CIO members who applauded the move very loudly.

It was against this background that there were widespread reports that some senior CIO officers continued to report to Mnangagwa after his departure from the CIO. A senior CIO officer, Rodgers Matongo, who was Assistant Director for Operations at the time, approached me and asked me to inform Dr. Sekeramayi that there were regular informal meetings taking place in Gweru during weekends, where the then Army Commander General Vitalis Zvinavashe, and some top CIO officers, were briefing Mnangagwa on State security matters. That was in 1992, long after Mnangagwa had left the CIO. Gweru is the provincial capital of the Midlands, the province which Mnangagwa has always regarded as his home and political base. Matongo added that some senior CIO officers openly declared their loyalty to Mnangagwa. I should point out that Zvinavashe had been very close to Mnangagwa since the days of the liberation war in Mozambique, when Zvinavashe served in the security portfolio as Mnangagwa's deputy. The friendship flourished after independence and appeared to have thrived against the background that the two came from the same geographical region of Masvingo/Midlands. General Zvinavashe succeeded General Mujuru as Commander of the Zimbabwe National Army in 1992, and got promoted to Commander of the Zimbabwe Defense Forces, but died some years later.

Being Assistant Director of Operations in the CIO at the time, Matongo had ample knowledge of security matters at the national level. Matongo explained to me that he could not report matters like that through the formal CIO hierarchy, because some of the senior officers through whose hands such a report would pass on the way up could be the pro-Mnangagwa officers who were taking part in the Gweru meetings. He wondered why the meetings were taking place in far-flung places like Gweru and why Mnangagwa, who was Justice Minister and not State Security Minister, was the one who was being briefed on national security matters in those briefings. He told me he suspected that Dr. Sekeramayi and President Mugabe were not privy to what was being discussed in those meetings. He also told me that it was obvious from the general mood among some senior CIO officers at

CIO headquarters, and from the Gweru meetings, that the CIO was continuing to be loyal to Mnangagwa, long after his departure from the CIO. He wondered what the implications were about the loyalty of Mnangagwa and the CIO to President Mugabe. Matongo died a disappointed man, from a car accident years later; he could not understand why President Mugabe and Dr. Sekeramayi seemed to underestimate the threat that Mnangagwa posed to Mugabe's government.

I briefed Dr. Sekeramayi in great detail about this matter. He had been aware of the pro-Mnangagwa sentiment in the CIO, but the alleged Gweru meetings surprised him. I would guess that Dr. Sekeramayi took this matter up with President Mugabe, however, at that stage I did not have the regular direct and confidential access to President Mugabe that I had in later years, and so I have no way of knowing what President Mugabe's reaction to reports about the Gweru meetings was.

I was worried that there continued to be loyalty to Mnangagwa among some senior CIO officers. I met regularly with Dr. Sekeramayi to discuss this matter with him and express my concerns. My advice was for him to make changes and move around CIO officers, to try to move those who were not loyal to peripheral positions, and move loyal officers into more critical areas. It was in that spirit that Dr. Sekeramayi appointed me a few years later to be Director of Administration, in charge of addressing the widespread discontent on an administrative level, which many CIO officers had since the time of Mnangagwa in the CIO.

Minister Sekeramayi drew considerable criticism from some CIO officers for keeping one Nothando Thuthani in his office in the position of staffing officer. While I was legal advisor, she advised the Minister on political issues and we both worked in the Minister's office reporting to him.

Nothando had been staffing officer to Mnangagwa while he was still Minister of State for National Security. It was widely rumoured, however, that Nothando was Mnangagwa's girlfriend and that the two of them had a child together. The indiscretion involved in Minister Sekeramayi keeping Nothando as his staffing officer was obvious and people in the CIO wondered why the Minister did not regard her as a security risk since Mnangagwa was still annoyed at being moved by President Mugabe away from the State Security portfolio.

Nothando was very close to July Moyo who worked at the Ministry of Labour and Social Welfare in the 1990s. They spent a lot of time together and one weekend on a Saturday evening they came together to my house in Harare to attend a graduation party that I was hosting for my sister. I knew that what kept them close was their political affiliation to Mnangagwa and that they both kept Mnangagwa informed about any information that could benefit Mnangagwa politically.

Nothando died in 2011. She had risen to the position of deputy director (external) in the CIO. July Moyo was appointed by Mnangagwa to Cabinet after the 2017 coup and remains one of Mnangagwa's senior Ministers.

MEANWHILE, THERE WAS armed conflict in Mozambique, with the Mozambique National Resistance (RENAMO) engaged in numerous skirmishes against the Mozambique government forces. The then president of Mozambique, Joachim Chissano, decided to explore a diplomatic initiative to end the war. He appointed President Mugabe and Kenyan President Daniel Arap Moi co- mediators, and entrusted to them the responsibility of bringing him and RENAMO leader Afonso Dhlakama together to negotiate an end to the war. President Mugabe appointed a Committee of Ministers to assist him, which consisted of Emmerson Mnangagwa, Dr. Sydney Sekeramayi and Richard Hove, who was Minister of Defense. The ministers in turn appointed a Committee of Officials to assist them, comprising Dr. Elleck Mashingaidze, who was Permanent Secretary for Foreign Affairs and was to become CIO Director General from 1992 to 1997, Edzai Chimonyo, who was a Brigadier at the time and later became Commander of the Zimbabwe National Army, Lieutenant-Colonel Mandebvu, and myself.

These committees started work in mid-1989. Typically, the way the committees worked was that members of the Zimbabwe committee of officials met their Kenyan counterparts and drew up a programme of action. The joint Zimbabwe-Kenya committee of officials then met officials of the Mozambican government and received instructions from them on peace proposals. The joint committee of officials then met RENAMO officials and presented to them the proposals from the Mozambican government. The Zimbabwe officials would then brief the Zimbabwe committee of ministers and President Mugabe, while the Kenyan side did the same on their side. The ministers and officials on both the Zimbabwe and Kenyan sides would then brief President Chissano on the developments on a regular basis, and so on.

Numerous meetings of this nature took place in Zimbabwe, Maputo, Nairobi, Rome, Blantyre and London between the years 1989 and 1992, when a peace agreement was finally signed in Rome, Italy, between President Chissano and Afonso Dhlakama, witnessed by Presidents Mugabe and Moi, as well as by the then South African Foreign Minister Pik Botha. The signing ceremony was hosted by the Saint Egidio Community, a lay Catholic community in Rome, which had become deeply involved during the late stages of the Mozambican peace talks.

It was during one of these numerous meetings that I noticed what I thought was remarkable about Mnangagwa, one day at Zimbabwe House. We had just come back from Nairobi as the committee of officials. Prior to this, we had been to Mozambique and President Chissano had a message for President Moi; he had asked that we convey the message directly to President Moi by word of mouth: in a nutshell, President Chissano was disgusted by the attitude of the then Kenyan Permanent Secretary for Foreign Affairs, Bethwell Kiplagat, who President

Chissano accused of betraying the Mozambican government's negotiating position by secretly disclosing it to RENAMO, and advising RENAMO on counter-offers to make. President Chissano wanted President Moi to read the riot act to Kiplagat and remove him from the Kenyan committee of officials.

We had arrived in Nairobi only to find that President Moi was out of town, and was at one of the State Houses in Eldoret. A road trip was arranged for us by Kenyan officials, and we duly met President Moi in Eldoret. President Moi, after receiving the message from President Chissano, wanted to consult President Mugabe, and he accordingly entrusted the Zimbabwe Committee of Officials with a message to be delivered to President Mugabe. Upon arrival in Harare from Nairobi, the Committee of Officials briefed the Committee of Ministers. During all our consultations and briefings as the Committee of Officials, Dr. Mashingaidze conducted the verbal briefings while I was responsible for taking notes, which Dr. Mashingaidze used as a reference in his verbal briefings.

After briefing the Committee of Ministers, a meeting to convey President Moi's message to President Mugabe was arranged. The meeting was set for one evening at Zimbabwe House, where President Mugabe resided at the time. That must have been in the year 1991. Zimbabwe House is situated in Harare opposite State House, which President Mugabe used for official and ceremonial functions. Members of the Committee of Ministers and of the

Committee of Officials promptly convened at Zimbabwe House for the meeting.

I had noticed that Mnangagwa often drove himself and did not like to be always driven, like other ministers did. Shortly after my arrival at Zimbabwe House, while still in the car park, Mnangagwa arrived, driving himself. One of the colleagues on the Committee of Officials whispered to me, and prompted me to look in the direction where Mnangagwa had parked his car; there was a young woman laying down on the back seat. Mnangagwa walked casually into Zimbabwe House and left the woman in the car. The colleague remarked that it took a lot of courage and disrespect for the President to bring a girlfriend into Zimbabwe House in the back of a car, like Mnangagwa had just done.

There had been talk in the CIO, in the aftermath of the 1988 cabinet reshuffle, that during his long tenure as Minister of State for National Security in the President's Office, Mnangagwa had become so powerful that President Mugabe had started to feel insecure and suspicious of his loyalty. This may explain Mnangagwa's removal from the CIO during the reshuffle, but apparently Mnangagwa maintained a high level of self-confidence even after his departure from the CIO, partly because of momentum, but also because he knew that he continued to secretly enjoy support and loyalty within the CIO.

A few weeks later, President Mugabe convened an emergency meeting of the ministers and officials involved in the Mozambican mediation process. The meeting was set for one afternoon at State House. We assembled at State House and were ushered into the office where President Mugabe was seated behind a desk. Present in the meeting were Ministers Mnangagwa, Sekeramayi, and Hove, as well as officials Dr. Mashingaidze, Brigadier Chimonyo, Lieutenant Colonel Mandebvu and myself. President Mugabe informed the meeting that he had received a telephone call from President Chissano, who had indicated that he had important information to share with him regarding recent covert meetings RENAMO had initiated, which were not consistent with the peace initiative the Mozambican government was pursuing. Furthermore, President Chissano had stressed the urgency of the matter, and he considered that it was important to meet the Zimbabwe delegation right away to discuss it. President Mugabe emphasized the need for the Zimbabwe delegation of ministers and officials present in the meeting to depart for Maputo right away, but wondered how that could be done since the Mozambican Airlines (LAM) flight had already departed for Maputo from Harare earlier that day.

Mnangagwa immediately interjected and informed President Mugabe that he could easily arrange transport for the delegation to be flown promptly to Maputo. President Mugabe looked surprised and asked Mnangagwa how he could do that. Mnangagwa replied that he had influential and wealthy friends who were willing and able to assist. He then told the meeting that he was confident that one such friend, Billy Rautenbach, would provide an aircraft to the delegation. President Mugabe looked relieved and impressed, and he immediately wound up the meeting and wished the delegation safe travel to Maputo. It was amazing to find, an hour later, a sleek private jet at the airport, with the label *"Wheels of Africa"*, ready to fly the delegation to Maputo. As the jet took off, Mnangagwa winked and boasted that he had wealthy friends, and told the delegation that the aircraft would be on standby, ready to fly the delegation back from Maputo to Harare at a moment's notice. That very same jet was to be made available again late in 1992, after the signing of the Mozambican peace agreement in Rome, when it flew not just the Zimbabwean delegation of ministers and officials, but President Mugabe as well. The signing ceremony and associated meetings ran late into the night, and the jet was very conveniently available to fly the delegation from Rome to London at around midnight. President Mugabe and his delegation were subsequently to take a connecting flight from London back to Harare. There is no doubt that Mnangagwa had again used his influence to make the jet available.

At that stage, I had begun to form the impression that Mnangagwa was assertive, fearless and decisive, but also corrupt and abrasive. It was becoming clear to me, from the many meetings I had attended, that President Mugabe regarded Mnangagwa as effective and efficient; it was evident that President Mugabe valued Mnangagwa's ability 'to get things done', and he liked Mnangagwa's results-oriented approach. Clearly, if President Mugabe was uncomfortable with the ethical aspects of how Mnangagwa got things done he did not show it. Moreover, Mnangagwa appeared to think that President Mugabe appreciated him so much that Mnangagwa felt confident enough to display some disrespect for President Mugabe at times during meetings. Typically, President Mugabe was feared by most ministers and officials. He was so much a disciplinarian that he required people attending his meetings to sit upright in chairs and not to relax in couches. I remember him remarking during a meeting at State House that couches are meant for those planning to take a nap, adding that those attending a meeting must sit upright in chairs. Yet, while typically participants in President Mugabe's meetings would show a high level of discipline and would be attentive, Mnangagwa would sometimes make jokes about the President. I remember Mnangagwa jokingly asking the president why he was always serious, when others like him often felt the need for jokes and laughter. I thought Mnangagwa had come to think that over the years he had impressed President Mugabe so much from his 'results-oriented approach', that President Mugabe now regarded him as indispensable.

IT WAS DURING one of the many visits to Nairobi by the committee of officials, around the year 1989/90, that General Edzai Chimonyo, who was a brigadier at the time (he was appointed Commander of the Zimbabwe National Army by Mnangagwa, after the November 2017 coup, but died a year or two later), started to discuss with Lieutenant- Colonel Mandebvu in my presence the relationship between General Solomon Mujuru and General Constantine Chiwenga. General Chimonyo said General Chiwenga was very angry with General Mujuru because General Chiwenga claimed that he had found General Mujuru's military uniform in his bedroom, which suggested that General Mujuru was having an affair with General Chiwenga's wife. General Chimonyo was debating with Lieutenant-Colonel Mandebvu whether there was substance in this claim by General Chiwenga. General Chiwenga was married to Jocelyn Chiwenga at the time.

This debate made me recall a day in the year 1988/89, when the then Permanent Secretary for Home Affairs, the late Tsomondo, was buried at his rural home in Hwedza, about two hundred kilometres south-east of Harare. I was still legal advisor in the CIO and junior to General Chiwenga, who was Major General then, but after the burial General Chiwenga invited me to ride in his car with him, back to Harare. He was chauffeur-driven, and I sat with General Chiwenga in the back seat all the way to Harare in his official Mercedes Benz vehicle. I formed the impression that General Chiwenga was a very sociable and simple person.

We arrived in Harare early in the evening, and General Chiwenga told the driver to drive to Colonel Tshinga Dube's house in Greendale. We spent about two hours in the colonel's house having drinks and snacks. Colonel Dube was the head of the Zimbabwe Defence Industries (Z.D.I.), an arms procurement arm of the Zimbabwe National Army, and was very close to General Mujuru. I am sure that at that time General Chiwenga and General Mujuru were still close, and I now wonder if the misunderstanding between them described by General Chimonyo made General Chiwenga turn away from General Mujuru toward Mnangagwa.

After a very nice evening at Colonel Dube's house in Greendale, General Chiwenga and I were driven to the General's house. I do not remember the location, but I think the house was in Borrowdale. The General was very pleasant and hospitable, and he invited me to have dinner with him. He introduced me to his wife, and I spent at least another two hours with them in their house. The General then instructed his driver to drive and drop me off at my house. I liked General Chiwenga very much for years after that, and paid a courtesy call on him at his office at the KGVI Barracks (later renamed Josiah Magama Tongogara Barracks) in Harare in 1998, when I became Deputy Director General in the CIO. However, I was disappointed later that year when I realized that General Chiwenga had become close friends with Shadreck Chipanga, who had become CIO Director General and with whom I was not on talking terms, because he regarded me as a political foe belonging to the Mujuru faction, while he was very close to Mnangagwa, who considered General Mujuru a political opponent.

MEANWHILE, A NUMBER of events were occurring outside the framework of the Mozambican mediation process, in which I had direct and indirect encounters with Mnangagwa.

In 1990, Patrick Kombayi was shot and seriously injured during parliamentary election campaigns in Gweru. Kombayi, now deceased, was a businessman, former mayor of Gweru, and Organizing Secretary for the Zimbabwe Unity Movement (ZUM), an opposition political party which was short-lived, and was led by Edgar Tekere, who had previously been ZANU (P.F.) Secretary General. Kombayi was contesting the Gweru urban parliamentary seat against the late Vice-President Simon Muzenda, who was standing on a ZANU (P.F.) ticket. Although he was seriously injured during the shooting, Kombayi survived the attack and went on to claim that he had been shot by Elias Kanengoni, the head of the CIO in the Midlands Province, and Kizito Chivamba, a senior ZANU (P.F.) Youth League official. Both Kanengoni and Chivamba are now deceased, but were then based in Gweru and were well-known to Kombayi at the time. The prosecution charged both Kanengoni and Chivamba a few months later with attempted murder.

I will point out at this stage that reports received by the CIO indicated that Kanengoni and Chivamba never shot Kombayi. Instead, Kombayi was shot by a CIO operative who was a bodyguard to Vice-President Muzenda. Kanengoni and Chivamba, who just happened to be present near the scene of the shooting, were well-known to Kombayi, and were considered by him political adversaries. They were at the scene observing the election campaign, in order to brief their principals – namely the CIO and ZANU (P.F.) – about how the election campaigns were unfolding.

In spite of strong denials of wrongdoing by Kanengoni and Chivamba, the Attorney General's Office (the forerunner to the National Prosecuting Authority) proceeded to charge and prosecute them. Kanengoni and Chivamba stood trial in the High Court in Bulawayo in 1992, and were both convicted of attempted murder and each sentenced to seven years in prison. They were briefly incarcerated at Khami Prison on the outskirts of Bulawayo – Zimbabwe's second-largest city – soon after their conviction, but released on bail pending appeal against both conviction and sentence. Their appeal in the Supreme Court in Harare a year later was dismissed.

I now explain the circumstances leading to the pardon which was granted by President Mugabe to Kanengoni and Chivamba, after the dismissal of their appeal by the Supreme Court. At the time of the shooting, confidential reports were compiled for President Mugabe by the CIO describing the circumstances surrounding Kombayi's shooting. The reports named the perpetrator of the shooting and were categorical that Kanengoni and Chivamba were not responsible for the shooting, as was being alleged by Kombayi and the media. These reports were shared with the Ministry of Home Affairs and the police, as well as the Attorney General's Office, which was the prosecuting authority. Patrick Chinamasa was the Attorney General responsible for criminal prosecutions at the time. The reports also alleged that Vice-President Muzenda,

Kombayi's competitor for the Gweru Urban parliamentary seat, at the very least, had knowledge of the plan to shoot Kombayi, and "looked the other way" because he stood to benefit from the elimination of competition for the Gweru urban parliamentary seat if Kombayi was shot and killed. Thus, there was a sensitive political dimension to the Kombayi shooting. In other words, had the real person responsible for the shooting of Kombayi been charged, the circumstances surrounding the shooting would have been in the public domain and would implicate Vice- President Muzenda. Since Kombayi alleged that it was Kanengoni and Chivamba who had shot him, it became convenient for Vice- President Muzenda and others to encourage that belief and push for their prosecution.

As Minister of Justice, Mnangagwa was perfectly placed to ensure that justice was done by prosecuting the correct people, but he did not do so. Mnangagwa was still nursing wounds from his removal from the CIO and did not wish his successor in the CIO, Dr. Sekeramayi, well. He sought to create an image problem for Dr. Sekeramayi by having the CIO, through Kanengoni, a senior CIO officer, associated with the shooting of Kombayi. The real perpetrator, a junior CIO officer and bodyguard, would have been acting under orders from Vice-President Muzenda, and so there would not have been an image problem for the CIO.

Moreover, Mnangagwa was aware that Vice-President Muzenda was the political godfather of Masvingo Province. Mnangagwa's political ambitions had always been tribally based, and he needed Muzenda's support to drive his political ambition of succeeding President Mugabe. Mnangagwa often claimed that after President Mugabe it was Masvingo's turn to provide the next leader of Zimbabwe, and he needed an alliance with Vice-President Muzenda to strengthen that claim. Protecting the Vice-President from prosecution in the Kombayi shooting was an excellent opportunity to do that. Muzenda's *quid pro quo* would be to assure Mnangagwa of political support in his presidential ambitions.

At that stage, reports had started surfacing that Mnangagwa was seeking to capture the judiciary and the prosecuting arm of the Attorney General's Office, for the purpose of using these State institutions as a weapon to fight political opponents. The strategy included influencing prosecutions to achieve political objectives. Chinamasa, as Attorney General, was known already to be very close to Mnangagwa (he was appointed Minister of Finance by Mnangagwa in the post-coup cabinet in November 2017). It was not surprising against that background that the prosecution of Kanengoni and Chivamba went ahead. Not only would the CIO headed by Dr. Sekeramayi be viewed nationwide as lawless, but officers and operatives in the CIO would be made to feel vulnerable if Kanengoni was convicted and sent to jail. They would feel unprotected and would agitate for a more assertive political head in the mould of Mnangagwa, who could protect them, unlike Dr. Sekeramayi.

I made arrangements for the CIO to pay for the legal representation of Kanengoni and Chivamba during their trial and appeal proceedings, and engaged Canaan Dube, who was with Kantor and Immerman at the time, to represent them, because I believed in their innocence. Dube was a friend who had been a classmate during the period I had studied law at the university, in 1977 and 1978. He had not joined the liberation war like I did, but had pursued his studies in law in West Africa until Zimbabwe's independence.

President Mugabe and Dr. Sekeramayi were aware of the plot to prosecute the wrong people for political reasons. The President was annoyed that his deputy Muzenda was working with Mnangagwa to create an image problem, because an image problem for Dr. Sekeramayi, who was a minister in the President's Office, amounted to an image problem for him. Dr. Sekeramayi asked me to recommend to him how to proceed in the event that the appeal by Kanengoni and Chivamba was unsuccessful. I advised that the way forward would be to recommend that President Mugabe pardon Kanengoni and Chivamba, but pointed out that the processing of an amnesty required the Minister of Justice to drive it. We both immediately anticipated resistance from Mnangagwa, who was Minister of Justice at the time.

On the day the appeal by Kanengoni and Chivamba was dismissed by the Supreme Court in 1993, Dr. Sekeramayi and I went to meet Mnangagwa at his office. I briefed Mnangagwa about the outcome of the appeal earlier that day. Dr. Sekeramayi then requested Mnangagwa to initiate the legal process for President Mugabe to pardon Kanengoni and Chivamba. Mnangagwa flatly refused and said that as Minister of Justice he stood by the decision of the Supreme Court. He added that he would not even accompany us to State House to discuss the matter with President Mugabe.

After the meeting, Dr. Sekeramayi told me to get ready to brief President Mugabe comprehensively about all the facts and legal issues surrounding the Kombayi shooting, and the Supreme Court's dismissal of the appeal by Kanengoni and Chivamba. At that point, Kanengoni and Chivamba were in hiding, as prison officers were after them. Dr. Sekeramayi arranged an urgent meeting for us with President Mugabe. An hour later we were at Zimbabwe House, and a long meeting took place involving just the three of us: that is, President Mugabe, Dr. Sekeramayi and myself. It was after that meeting that President Mugabe pardoned Kanengoni and Chivamba.

A MATTER WHICH made Mnangagwa controversial was that during his long tenure as Minister of State for National Security in the President's Office, he kept a fairly large number of white officers serving the CIO in senior and very sensitive positions. The most notable one was Danny Stannard, who was Director of the Internal Branch of the CIO. Most intelligence matters on what was going on in Zimbabwe passed through his hands, and the only people who were more senior to him in the CIO were the Director General and the Minister.

There was a lot of concern about this state of affairs in the CIO. Zimbabwe was facing serious security threats from

South Africa at the time, with the South African apartheid regime showing open hostility toward the Zimbabwe government. The apartheid government suspected that the Zimbabwe government was harbouring members of Umkhonto we Sizwe, the military arm of the African National Congress (A.N.C.), which was fighting against the apartheid South African government. The apartheid government remained in place in South Africa until 1994, when a democratic government led by Nelson Mandela replaced it.

In Zimbabwe, the Public Service Commission was deliberately retiring some white officers and replacing them with blacks, especially in sensitive senior positions, to ensure that the civil service was loyal to the Zimbabwe government. Many people in government in Zimbabwe expected the CIO to take the lead in that policy, in view of the sensitivity of its mandate, and were surprised that the CIO was instead lagging far behind.

Matters came to a head in 1988, when a house occupied by members of the A.N.C. was bombed, resulting in the death of one Obert Mwanza. Mwanza was a Zambian who had been recruited for the attack by the bombers, but died accidentally while detonating a bomb remotely. The house was in Trenance, a suburb in Bulawayo in western Zimbabwe, and was unoccupied at the time of the attack.

In November 1988, the High Court in Harare sentenced three men to death in connection with the attack and the death of Mwanza. They were John Kevin Woods, a member of the CIO, Michael Smith, who had been a soldier in the Rhodesian Light Infantry, and Phillip Conjwayo, who had served in the Rhodesian police's Special Branch. Woods and Smith were white, while Conjwayo was black. Testimony during the trial was clear that the three men were spies for the South African apartheid government, and that the attack was meant to eliminate A.N.C. fighters who were suspected to have been occupying the house in Trenance. The three men were sent to Chikurubi Maximum Security Prison on the outskirts of Harare, on death row.

The attack highlighted among many in the Zimbabwe government the folly of retaining white officers in the CIO in senior positions, like Mnangagwa had done. At that stage, Mnangagwa had left the CIO and was now Minister of Justice, so it became Dr. Sekeramayi's responsibility to deal with the matter and consider what corrective action to take. In pursuit of that objective, Dr. Sekeramayi sought to find out the extent to which the South African apartheid government had infiltrated the Zimbabwe government, and had spies in Zimbabwe government structures working for it.

It was with that objective in mind that sometime in 1991 Dr. Sekeramayi came up with a plan to offer Woods, Smith and Conjwayo their freedom, if they cooperated and disclosed to the Zimbabwe government all they knew about the South African apartheid government's espionage operations and networks in Zimbabwe. In that connection, Dr. Sekeramayi took me one morning to Mnangagwa's office, and requested Mnangagwa to facilitate my visit to Chikurubi Maximum Security Prison, to "have a chat" with John Kevin Woods, Michael Smith and Phillip Conjwayo. The administration of prisons in Zimbabwe falls under the Minister of Justice, and so Mnangagwa was the appropriate authority to give clearance for such a visit. Mnangagwa was taken aback and not enthusiastic about the plan, but grudgingly gave his permission.

A few days later the visit was arranged, and I drove into Chikurubi Maximum Security Prison one afternoon on my own. The prison complex is an enormous structure with several barriers, but I passed through all the gates with relative ease, until I got to a waiting room with benches. I was asked to wait for a few minutes in the room while the prisoners were being summoned for the interview.

About half an hour later the three men were brought into the room. They had overgrown beards and were in death row prison uniform. They looked suspiciously at me and Woods looked quite hostile. In spite of my repeated assurances that they would walk out of the prison as free men in a day or two if they cooperated, the three men all emphatically refused to cooperate and swore their unwavering loyalty to the South African apartheid government. They were convinced that the apartheid government would one day save them.

This outcome of the visit to Chikurubi Maximum Security Prison served to confirm the fears that the South African apartheid government had their spies deeply embedded within the Zimbabwe government. The need for a more rapid transformation of the leadership in the CIO became obvious and it was against that background that Dr. Sekeramayi initiated a policy to retire from the CIO senior officers whose loyalty to the Zimbabwe government was in doubt. Danny Stannard and a number of other senior white officers were gradually phased out of the CIO on retirement, in the next two to three years.

There was quite a loud outcry among the remnants of the pro- Mnangagwa officers in the CIO, criticizing these changes. This was surprising and disturbing in view of the fact that these officers appeared to be condoning the destabilization activities by the South African apartheid government, against the government of President Mugabe.

It appeared difficult to imagine that, for all his apparent revolutionary past, Mnangagwa could have been affiliated to elements in the apartheid South African regime. This appeared to be consistent with the observation by some security analysts that Mnangagwa received active military and intelligence assistance from white officers and mercenaries, who had fought on the side of the Rhodesian security forces against the liberation forces of Zimbabwe, when he co-ordinated the military operations in western Zimbabwe which resulted in massacres of civilians in the early 1980s.

MY CAREER IN the CIO was to take a dramatic turn in 1993. In August of that year Eddison Shirihuru, who had been Deputy Director General in the CIO, died. Shirihuru had been the leading police suspect in the disappearance in May 1990 of Rashiwe Guzha, who had been a typist at the Treasury Computer Bureau in Harare. There appeared to have been a romantic relationship between her and Shirihuru before her disappearance. The police portfolio fell under the Ministry of Home Affairs. When police investigations into her disappearance started to point to Shirihuru, I met Tinaye Chigudu, a deputy secretary in the Ministry of Home Affairs, to discuss the implications. Shirihuru was senior to me in the CIO, but as legal advisor I wanted the CIO to take a position on the matter.

The Minister of Home Affairs at the time was Dumiso Dabengwa. I knew that Dabengwa had been detained without trial for years under the state of emergency in the 1980s, during the time of the Gukurahundi massacres in Matabeleland and Midlands Provinces. He had been accused of being leader of the dissidents who had taken up arms against President Mugabe's government. Mnangagwa was Minister of State for National Security at the time and had worked closely with Shirihuru, who was already a senior CIO officer, to keep Dabengwa behind bars indefinitely, in spite of court orders ordering Dabengwa's release.

The history behind this was that the liberation war in Zimbabwe was fought mainly by two political parties, namely ZANU and ZAPU (Zimbabwe African People's Union). ZANU's military wing was the Zimbabwe African National Liberation Army (ZANLA), while ZAPU's military wing was the Zimbabwe People's Revolutionary

Army (ZIPRA). ZANU was mainly sponsored by China while ZAPU was sponsored by the Soviet Union, now Russia. ZANLA fought from military bases in neighbouring Mozambique, while ZIPRA fought from neighbouring Zambia. Dumiso Dabengwa was the intelligence chief of ZIPRA and fought alongside Lookout Masuku, who was the ZIPRA military commander.

After the signing of the Lancaster House Conference in 1979, Frontline States pushed ZAPU leader Joshua Nkomo and ZANU leader Robert Mugabe to contest the elections which were coming in 1980 as a united political front. The Frontline States was a political grouping of independent southern African states which were pushing for the liberation of Zimbabwe and Namibia, and the end of apartheid in South Africa. The group comprised Presidents Julius Nyerere of Tanzania, Samora Moises Machel of Mozambique, Kenneth Kaunda of Zambia and Jose Eduardo dos Santos of Angola. ZAPU and ZANU agreed to contest the elections as a united front and that gave birth to ZANU (P.F.), with P.F. standing for "Patriotic Front". Thus, ZANU and ZAPU had united in order to contest the elections in 1980 as a united front known as ZANU (P.F.). However, ZANU President Robert Mugabe reneged on the agreement and decided that ZANU would contest the elections separately from ZAPU. That created animosity between the two parties. ZANU went on to win the 1980 elections and formed the government with Mugabe as prime minister. There was an exercise to integrate the three armies after independence

– namely ZANLA, ZIPRA and the Rhodesian army – but some ZIPRA members started pulling out of the integrated army, alleging discrimination against them. That was the beginning of the disturbances in the western Matabeleland provinces in Zimbabwe in the early 1980s. The government arrested and detained Lookout Masuku and Dumiso Dabengwa, and accused them of leading the war by ZIPRA dissidents fighting the new government. They spent up to four years in prison, and Masuku died a month after his release in April 1986. The men were released toward the time of the signing of a unity agreement between ZAPU and ZANU, which saw the birth of the united party ZANU (P.F.) in 1987, bringing to an end the disturbances in the Matabeleland and Midlands provinces.

When I met Chigudu in 1993, there was at the back of my mind the suspicion that there might be a vindictive attitude in the Ministry of Home Affairs, driven by a revenge motive on the part of Dabengwa against Shirihuru. Chigudu confirmed to me that police investigations were progressing and Shirihuru was the leading suspect in Rashiwe Guzha's disappearance. He thought that it was a question of time before Shirihuru was charged with kidnapping Guzha. At that stage, Shirihuru was being interrogated from time to time by the Police Criminal Investigations Department (C.I.D.) Homicide Section in connection with not only kidnapping, but the suspected murder of Guzha, as well.

I reported to Dr. Sekeramayi what Chigudu had told me, and advised that in the circumstances it was appropriate for the minister to suspend Shirihuru from the CIO until the police investigations were completed. The minister agreed and suspended Shirihuru from the CIO in May 1993. Shirihuru was in his late sixties at the time, and was diabetic and had other health issues. He at times drank heavily, and at one time he had staggered into President Mugabe's hotel suite in a drunken stupor, after drinking whisky during one of the President's foreign visits. President Mugabe had been shocked seeing Shirihuru in such a drunken state, and had banned Shirihuru from accompanying him on his foreign trips for months. The police investigations, Shirihuru's health issues, his age, his occasional excessive drinking, and his suspension from the CIO must have combined to take a serious toll on him; Shirihuru collapsed and died at his home in Cranborne, Harare in August 1993.

Shirihuru had been a very senior security advisor to President Mugabe for years in his position as Deputy Director General in the CIO, and travelled with the President on most of his visits to foreign countries. He briefed President Mugabe on security matters on a daily basis. As he had become very close to the President and, because of his very assertive nature, Shirihuru sometimes had instant audience with the President. He was known to the President's secretarial staff as one of the very few officials who could demand this. Shirihuru had also worked very closely with Mnangagwa while the latter headed the CIO. Mnangagwa often fondly called him "Big Bird", a literal translation of the Shona word "Shirihuru". Shirihuru had been promoted by Mnangagwa to the position of Deputy Director General in the CIO.

Shirihuru had been very well-connected, even in business circles. I remember one evening at a hotel in Bindura, north of Harare – while on a business trip with Shirihuru and a few other senior CIO officers – being hosted by James Makamba, who was a prominent businessman and former radio disc jockey. Makamba had worked for Lonrho, a London-based conglomerate which used to be run by Tiny Rowland; Makamba worked closely with Tiny Rowland for years. Makamba spent the evening having drinks with us and arranged a dinner of home-cooked goat meat for us. He appeared to be close to Shirihuru. In the early 1990s, Shirihuru also introduced me to the managing director of Barclays Zimbabwe, Isaac Takawira, who assisted me to obtain a loan from the bank.

At Shirihuru's funeral at his home village near Murehwa, President Mugabe delivered a highly combative and emotional eulogy. He praised Shirihuru's loyalty and dedication to duty. The President also spoke about the police investigations, and said no evidence had ever been provided to him linking Shirihuru to Rashiwe Guzha's disappearance.

I did not hear much about the circumstances surrounding the disappearance of Rashiwe Guzha, except for media reports and rumours within CIO, alleging that Shirihuru was responsible for her disappearance. However, Ernest Tekere told me of a very intriguing telephone conversation he had with Shirihuru, which may have been connected to the disappearance.

Tekere was the provincial head of the CIO, and was based in Bulawayo. Tekere and I had been classmates in the 1970s at Kwenda Mission, about 40 kilometres east of Chivhu town. He went on to join the Rhodesian Special Branch, a paramilitary police unit which operated together with the Rhodesian army against freedom fighters, during Zimbabwe's liberation war in the 1970s. From Kwenda Mission I had gone on to Hartzell High School and then to the University of Rhodesia, as the University of Zimbabwe was then known, and on to Mozambique during the last two years of Zimbabwe's liberation war, which I participated in. I had met Tekere again after I became legal adviser to Minister Sekeramayi in 1988, when my duties took me to provincial CIO offices regularly. One day, sometime in 1995, after I had become the Director of Administration in CIO, I travelled by road with Tekere from Victoria Falls to Bulawayo. Tekere was driving and there were only the two of us in the car. Shirihuru had died in 1993. I started asking Tekere what he thought about the allegations that Shirihuru had been behind the disappearance and possibly death of Rashiwe Guzha. Tekere claimed that he did not know if there was any substance behind the allegations, but then started narrating a telephone conversation he'd had with Shirihuru. Tekere told me that during the days when the police were interviewing Shirihuru in connection with Rashiwe Guzha's disappearance, Shirihuru called him one day in early 1993. During the telephone call, Shirihuru ordered Tekere to hunt down a buffalo, cut off its head and put the head in a plastic bag, which he had to tie tightly, so that the buffalo head would remain warm for hours. Tekere was to then drive from Bulawayo to Harare – a distance of some 450 kilometres – and give the plastic bag to Shirihuru, while the buffalo head was still warm. Shirihuru had emphasized that the buffalo head would only be useful to him if he got it while it was still warm.

Tekere told me that he thought Shirihuru wanted the buffalo head for ritual purposes. He suspected that Shirihuru may have been involved in the killing of someone and wanted to appease the spirit of the dead person, which may have started haunting him. It was obvious from my conversation with Tekere that he thought the dead person may have been Rashiwe Guzha.

Tekere said that he complied with Shirihuru's instructions, and delivered the buffalo head to him at his home in Harare, while it was still warm.

In later years, after I had left CIO, Tekere was reported by the media in Zimbabwe to have directed a CIO operation which produced damning video evidence of a sexual nature, showing Archbishop Pius Ncube's involvement in sexual acts with married women. Ncube had been a vocal critic of President Mugabe's human rights record. Tekere's video evidence compromised Archbishop Pius Ncube so much that he was disgraced and forced to resign. That must have been an enormous relief to Mugabe, and Tekere may have been generously rewarded by the Mugabe regime for the sting operation.

I did not hear about Tekere again until early 2021, when the Zimbabwe media reported that he had committed suicide.

In December 1993, Dr. Sekeramayi and Dr. Elleck Mashingaidze, who had become CIO Director General in 1992, appointed a successor to Shirihuru. The new appointee to the position of Deputy Director General was Shadreck Chipanga, who had been Director of Administration in the CIO. At the same time, I was appointed to succeed Chipanga as Director of Administration. That is how Shirihuru's death in 1993 dramatically impacted my career in the CIO.

Chipanga had previously been Director of External Operations in the CIO. He was an ex-detainee and was very close to Mnangagwa. He was a strong advocate of emergency powers which had allowed police and security officers to detain people without trial, and had been unhappy with my contrary views on the matter.

As Director of Administration, he had presided over a network of officers who had a strong affiliation to Mnangagwa. Many CIO officers complained that they were being discriminated against by Chipanga's pro-Mnangagwa network, by being denied promotion and benefits. Dr. Sekeramayi and Dr. Mashingaidze informed me upon my appointment that they expected me to address these complaints. I agreed to do so, but expressed my anxiety about the promotion of Chipanga to the position of Deputy Director General. He would be senior to me, and it appeared to me that confrontation with him would be unavoidable when I started dismantling the pro- Mnangagwa network he had presided over.

While he was Director of External Operations, Chipanga had recommended the appointment of Pearson Mbalekwa to a diplomatic position in Nairobi, Kenya. It turned out that Mbalekwa was Mnangagwa's close relative. Mbalekwa was to continue to be elevated and sponsored by the pro-Mnangagwa network until he became a member of Parliament a few years later, and would engage in public political battles against political opponents like me in Parliament under the protection of parliamentary privilege.

I point out at this stage that in the late 1990s there was extensive media coverage of a political battle linked to President Mugabe's succession between a "Mnangagwa faction" and a "Mujuru faction". Dr. Sekeramayi was believed to belong to the Mujuru faction and I was perceived by Chipanga and Mnangagwa to belong to the Mujuru faction, since I worked closely with Dr. Sekeramayi. The Mnangagwa faction actively supported Mnangagwa's ambition to succeed Mugabe as President, while the Mujuru faction was opposed to Mnangagwa's political ambitions and regarded him as unfit to become President. In this connection, Mbalekwa was assigned by Chipanga and Mnangagwa to make public attacks in Parliament against my integrity, in order to undermine the Mujuru faction's credibility. This is elaborated later in Part Three.

I felt very anxious about the wisdom of the promotion of Chipanga, and started to doubt Dr. Sekeramayi's prospects of success in turning the CIO's loyalty away from Mnangagwa if he was promoting people like Chipanga, who were loyal to Mnangagwa. I had often heard Chipanga boast that he enjoyed the confidence of President Mugabe, because they had been in prison together as political detainees. Like Mnangagwa, President Mugabe was said to value acquaintances made in prison during political detention. I believe key people like Mnangagwa and Chipanga exploited that attitude and feigned unwavering support to President Mugabe while pursuing their own political ambitions.

In January 1994 I took up the position of Director of Administration in the CIO, and immediately set out to address the grievances of the rank and file in the CIO, in the firm belief that I had the backing of Dr. Sekeramayi as Minister and Dr. Mashingaidze as Director General. My immediate boss was Dr. Mashingaidze; I reported through him to Dr. Sekeramayi.

CIO middle- and lower-ranking officers were complaining about an unfair promotion process, a punitive, unfair and discriminatory disciplinary process, and the absence in the CIO of initiatives aimed at improving their welfare. They alleged that during Chipanga's time in the CIO administration one's position and welfare in the organization depended on whether they came from the Midlands /Masvingo provinces or not. Loyalty to Mnangagwa was the important factor which determined whether one was eligible for promotion or enjoyed other favourable outcomes in the CIO, not merit.

I turned around the disgruntlement in the CIO by reassigning heads of divisions in administration, and placing in key areas qualified and competent officers who had the welfare of officers at heart. I also ensured that there was a paradigm shift at that senior level regarding fairness, and the need to improve the welfare not just of senior members of the organization, but of middle and lower- ranking members as well. These efforts brought about immediate praise and raised the morale in the organization to levels never witnessed before. Dr. Sekeramayi and Dr. Mashingaidze were highly commended by the rank and file, and they encouraged me to stay the course. However, there was resentment by the pro-Mnangagwa network, and opposition to these efforts by that network became more pronounced and bolder with time.

I discussed with Dr. Mashingaidze the budgetary constraints the organization was facing. Dr. Mashingaidze and I regularly met Treasury officials to discuss the CIO's financial needs, when the officials stressed to us the budgetary constraints that government as a whole was facing, and made it clear to us that the CIO was equally impacted. I suggested to Dr. Mashingaidze that if the organization was to have the capacity to continue to improve the welfare of its rank and file, and to conduct its operations effectively, there was a need to consider innovative initiatives by the organization aimed at strengthening its financial capacity. It was against that background that Dr. Mashingaidze and

I proposed to Dr. Sekeramayi a business initiative for the CIO which involved the organization's entry into the real estate business, through a CIO-owned private company formed specifically for the purpose. The investment would start off as a modest one, but would grow over time as the profits made were re-invested. The Minister approved the request and the project was implemented from the beginning of 1995. Not surprisingly, the pro-Mnangagwa network in the CIO was to engage in a public disinformation campaign against the initiative, and would find it convenient to allege that there were corrupt motives on my part in initiating the investment.

In the year 1997 Dr. Mashingaidze lost his eyesight. His deputy Chipanga had been the focal point of the resistance to the initiatives that Dr. Mashingaidze and I had been pursuing, to improve the welfare of the rank and file in the CIO and to improve its effectiveness. Dr. Mashingaidze and I had shared the vision that government needed a CIO with competent, professional and well-looked after officers to ensure that its advice to government was of a high quality and was valuable. However, Chipanga had the attitude that these initiatives were aimed at discrediting him since, as my predecessor in the position of Director of Administration, he had not come up with any initiatives to improve the welfare of officers; instead there had been widespread discontent during his time. Thus Chipanga was coordinating the resistance by the pro-Mnangagwa network to the new initiatives, but Dr. Mashingaidze had been overriding him in his efforts.

Dr. Mashingaidze could not continue as CIO Director General after becoming blind, and he was retired by President Mugabe in November 1997. In the period leading to his becoming blind, Dr. Mashingaidze had fallen victim to adverse media publicity arising from what appeared to be the work of political enemies. In the year 1995, local weekly newspaper *The Financial Gazette* ran a story disclosing that President Mugabe had started a romantic relationship while still married to Sally Mugabe. This was a reference to the relationship between the President and Grace Marufu, whom the President later married and who became Zimbabwe's First Lady. The relationship started secretively before Sally Mugabe's death in 1992, and they had their wedding in 1996. The newspaper was charged with criminal defamation in connection with leaking the details about the relationship. The author of the newspaper story, Simbarashe Makunike, claimed in court that the story was leaked to him by Dr. Mashingaidze while he was Director General of the

CIO. However, the court believed the testimony by Dr. Mashingaidze that he never discussed the matter with Makunike, and convicted Makunike of criminal defamation.

This claim by Makunike was devastating to Dr. Mashingaidze, as it implied that he was not loyal to President Mugabe. As Director General of the CIO he was the custodian of State secrets, and was expected to have unwavering loyalty to the President; accusations of leaking secrets to do with the President's personal life amounted to an act of betrayal. Dr. Mashingaidze was diabetic, and it is very likely that the stress brought about by the false claims by Makunike worsened his health condition and accelerated his progression toward blindness. This may have been a deliberate act by Dr. Mashingaidze's enemies. As I elaborate below, the pro-Mnangagwa network in the CIO ran a network of journalists in the public and private media whose task was to push Mnangagwa's political agenda and destroy the reputation of political opponents. It is highly likely that Makunike was one such journalist, who probably worked with Chipanga to destroy Dr Mashingaidze's career in the CIO. Chipanga stood to gain from the intrigue by being elevated to the position of CIO Director General at Dr. Mashingaidze's exit from the CIO due to blindness. Moreover, as CIO Director General Chipanga would be well-placed to push Mnangagwa's political agenda and political ambitions.

I was shocked when Chipanga was appointed to replace Dr. Mashingaidze as CIO Director General in December 1997. I would now be reporting to Chipanga, and I knew I would not have his support in anything I did. I offered to resign immediately from the CIO, but the Minister turned down my resignation. We sat down in his office and I expressed my disappointment to Dr. Sekeramayi that Chipanga, who had been the leader of the pro-Mnangagwa network in the CIO, had now become the CIO Director General. I reminded the Minister that he and Dr. Mashingaidze had in 1993 appointed me Director of Administration and had specifically tasked me to reverse the discriminatory policies that Chipanga had pursued in that position, which had caused an outcry in the organization. I could not understand how the Minister and President Mugabe had now found Chipanga suitable for even higher office. I reminded the Minister that Chipanga was openly pro-Mnangagwa and his loyalty to the President was in doubt. I wondered how that made him suitable to be CIO Director General.

Dr. Sekeramayi asked me to reconsider my decision to resign. He told me that President Mugabe had just gone away on annual leave and would be away until the end of January 1998. Dr. Sekeramayi said that upon President Mugabe's resumption of duty in February 1998, he would be recommending to the President my appointment as Deputy Director General, thereby deputizing Chipanga. The Minister felt that as his deputy I would have the capacity to fend off any attempts by Chipanga to victimize me.

In early February 1998 Dr. Sekeramayi convened a meeting of CIO directors, which was also attended by Chipanga as the CIO Director General. In that meeting Dr. Sekeramayi introduced me as the new Deputy Director General. Chipanga was completely taken by surprise and could not hide his opposition to my appointment. He told the meeting that the appointment was a complete shock to him and he considered it inappropriate, because there were directors in the CIO who were more senior to me, as they had been directors for a much longer period than me. I was surprised that Chipanga could openly oppose an appointment made by President Mugabe and Dr.

Sekeramayi. Both Director General and Deputy Director General of the CIO are positions appointed by the State President on the advice of the Minister of State for National Security in the President's Office. I immediately started to expect hostility from Chipanga in the discharge of my duties as CIO Deputy Director General.

AS CIO DEPUTY Director General I attended President Mugabe's morning briefings and briefed him on security matters in private, before or after the main morning briefing. Police Commissioner General Augustine Chihuri briefed the President once a week in private while I briefed him on a daily basis, whenever there were matters of security interest to bring to his attention. I also accompanied the President on his visits to various parts of the country as well as on most of his foreign visits. During his visit to any foreign country I would brief him about any events or developments taking place back in Zimbabwe in his absence, with a focus on the security aspects of those events. Chipanga sought to make my work impossible by withholding classified reports and other intelligence from me, but I cultivated a very useful network of CIO officers which kept me informed about matters that were of security interest to the President.

A few months after my appointment there started to appear in some newspapers in Zimbabwe negative reports about me. The reports alleged that while still Director of Administration I had engaged in corrupt deals which benefitted me personally, and that I had misappropriated huge amounts of money. It soon became obvious that

Chipanga was behind these allegations in the media, in an effort to destroy my integrity. It became apparent that the pro-Mnangagwa network in the CIO had contacts in the media, whom they used to publish adverse stories against perceived political opponents. A reporter for The Financial Gazette, Kindness Paradza, incessantly wrote articles in the paper with a pro-Mnangagwa bias and alleged that I had been engaged in massive corrupt deals in the CIO. It was soon in the public domain that there were serious power struggles at the top level in the CIO, and that the issue of who was likely to succeed President Mugabe was at the centre of the power struggle.

The power struggle, as reported by the media at the time, involved a "Mnangagwa faction" which was aspiring to take over from President Mugabe, but was being challenged by a "Mujuru faction", which was led by the late General Solomon Mujuru. In a nutshell, Mnangagwa was aspiring to succeed President Mugabe and had created a network of key officials in the CIO, the Public Service, other security organs and the Judiciary, to assist him to push his political ambition. The network included key officials like Dr. Meshack Sibanda in the Office of the President and Cabinet, Chipanga in the CIO, a number of judges, a number of journalists and some senior members of the defense forces. Mnangagwa knew that he lacked the charisma to win elections, either at the ruling party congress to become party leader, or to win national presidential elections, and so this network of people loyal to him was meant to eventually propel him to power in an undemocratic manner. Thus, the idea of a coup in one form or another against Mugabe by Mnangagwa started way back in the 1980s. General Mujuru was the figurehead and "kingmaker" of the other faction, but was in fact supporting the candidature of Dr. Sekeramayi to succeed President Mugabe.

It was against that background that an intense media onslaught against me took place in 1998, while I was Deputy Director General. Chipanga and the pro-Mnangagwa faction regarded me as being close to Dr. Sekeramayi, and so I was seen as belonging to the Mujuru faction. The negative media publicity I suffered at the hands of the likes of Kindness Paradza was a political onslaught by the Mnangagwa faction, directed against the Mujuru faction. Kindness Paradza was rewarded by Mnangagwa for his efforts by being made chair of a Parliamentary Portfolio Committee in the Mnangagwa government, after the November 2017 coup, and was subsequently appointed deputy Minister of Information by Mnangagwa.

As part of this media onslaught against me, *The Financial Gazette* in 1998 published details about the dwelling house I was building in my hometown of Chivhu, complete with the picture of the double-storey house. The paper alleged that the house was being built with the proceeds of the corrupt deals I had engaged in. However, in subsequent editions of the newspaper it was claimed that the house in fact belonged to First Lady Grace Mugabe, and that the two of us were related. The former First Lady comes from Chivhu, but we are not related. The intention behind the publication and the false claims was to cause a rift between me and the First Lady.

I received a telephone call from the First Lady on the day of the publication of those claims, and she was demanding to know how she was being linked to a house that did not belong to her. We arranged to meet and I met her the same day, in her office at Zimbabwe House. She was convinced after our meeting that this was the work of people who were fighting political battles. She was aware of the negative media publicity I was receiving at the time, and she quickly attributed the publication to the battles to succeed President Mugabe which were going on.

So fierce was the media attack against me that it became obvious that the leadership at the CIO had become paralyzed, with Chipanga and myself completely unable to work together. This is reflected in the following article of 14th December 2000, from *The New Humanitarian* (formerly IRIN News):

"...(CIO) officers interviewed by 'The Financial Gazette' this week said the factionalism which began during Chipanga's time, and saw officers splitting and aligning themselves to different camps of Zimbabwean politicians, had been difficult to eradicate. The officers said politicians secretly vying for the presidency regarded the CIO as a big centre for power, and many of the politicians were eager to exert influence on the organization..."

The main message in the media onslaught against me by the Mnangagwa faction was that I was corrupt and had misappropriated CIO funds to benefit myself. The Mnangagwa faction has over the years acquired a reputation of claiming to be virtuous while destroying the image of political opponents. They accuse opponents of being what they in fact are themselves. I quote from an interview of Dr. Jonathan Moyo in February 2020, by Itai Mushekwe of *Spotlight Zimbabwe:*

"There's more about him (Mnangagwa). If you point out his murderous record, he'll seek to silence you by getting his cronies to falsely accuse you of being a murderer; if you expose his looting history, he'll unleash his minnows to accuse you of being a thief. This is because Mnangagwa has no moral compass that enables him to tell right from wrong."

I find this quote to be an accurate description of the behaviour of Mnangagwa and his associates at the time they launched a media onslaught against me in 1998. Dr. Jonathan Moyo was Minister of Information and Publicity in President Mugabe's cabinet in the early 2000s and Minister of Higher and Tertiary Education at the time President Mugabe was overthrown by Mnangagwa, in the November 2017 military coup.

I discussed these matters with Dr. Sekeramayi several times but I did not sense that a solution to my conflict with Chipanga was in sight. I then privately raised the matter with President Mugabe. The President asked me what Chipanga's fight with me was all about and I explained to him that Chipanga was fighting a political battle on behalf of Mnangagwa against me, because their perception was that I belonged to the Mujuru faction, their political adversary. The President asked if I had discussed the matter with Dr. Sekeramayi. I told the President that I had done so but I was unsure if the Minister took the matter seriously. President Mugabe then suddenly asked me: "Do you think he may be conniving?"

I told the President that I thought Dr. Sekeramayi may indeed be conniving with the Mnangagwa faction. I told the President that I had even raised my concerns with Vice-President Simon Muzenda, who had shown no surprise and had remarked that Dr. Sekeramayi had the reputation of "having his household run for him by others", unlike people like Dr. Ushewokunze, who were assertive and always had a hands-on approach. Dr. Herbert Ushewokunze was a cabinet minister in President Mugabe's cabinet for years. I had not pursued the matter with Vice-President Muzenda because I knew he was supporting Mnangagwa in his political ambitions.

President Mugabe did not say if he was going to take action in connection with the matter. I was concerned that the President appeared to underestimate the threat posed by the Mnangagwa faction to his presidency. There were reports that some of the key people in his office such as Dr. Meshack Sibanda were closely related to Mnangagwa and were loyal to him. Dr. Sibanda was deputy to Dr. Charles Utete, who was Secretary to the President and Cabinet in the Mugabe administration. In that position, Dr. Sibanda had full access to all the sensitive information in government and if he was loyal to Mnangagwa, who had strong presidential ambitions, then Mnangagwa probably had access to all classified government information through Dr. Sibanda in the same way that President Mugabe had. Chipanga also had access to top secret information as CIO Director General, and his loyalty to Mnangagwa also ought to have worried President Mugabe. In fact, Dr Sibanda was to serve in the Mnangagwa administration after the 2017 coup in the top government position of Chief Secretary to the President and Cabinet.

I met a number of influential people seeking their assistance in influencing President Mugabe and Dr. Sekeramayi to resolve the problem of my difficult working relationship with Chipanga. One of the people was Air Chief Marshall Perence Shiri, who I met at his office at K.G. VI Barracks (later renamed Josiah Magama Tongogara Barracks). Shiri had earlier in 1998 met me in the Robert Mugabe International Airport V.I.P. lounge, just before I boarded a flight accompanying President Mugabe to London, and had asked me to suggest to President Mugabe to appoint General Solomon Mujuru as Minister of Defense. I could sense from the suggestion that senior military commanders were unhappy with the then Minister of Defense, Moven Mahachi, who was rumoured in military circles to be ineffective. I had conveyed the message to President Mugabe during a private meeting in his hotel suite in London, but he did not appear enthusiastic about the idea. When I met Shiri in connection with my problems with Chipanga he suggested that I discuss the matter with General Mujuru and, since the General was close to Dr. Sekeramayi, Shiri thought that the General could persuade Dr. Sekeramayi to intervene.

I should point out that as things looked in the year 1998, General Mujuru appeared close to both General Chiwenga and Air Chief Marshall Shiri. General Mujuru was Mnangagwa's bitter political rival, yet General Chiwenga and Air Marshall Shiri went on to be appointed Vice-President and cabinet minister respectively in Mnangagwa's administration, after the November 2017 military coup. It does not add up. I suspect that the explanation lies in the events in Matabeleland in the early 1980s, during the period of the Gukurahundi massacres, when up to 20,000 civilians were massacred by the Zimbabwe National Army. Although I do not have a first-hand account of those events, because I was in the diplomatic service in Mozambique and Romania 1980-1983, and in full-time study at the University of Zimbabwe 1984-1986, press reports indicate that Air Chief Marshall Shiri was the Commander of the Fifth Brigade of the Zimbabwe National Army which committed the atrocities, that General Chiwenga was Commander of a brigade which also operated in Matabeleland during that time, and that some senior people in the CIO – like Shirihuru, Chipanga and Maynard Muzariri (a director in the CIO who later became Deputy Director General, but died in 2011) – were also involved in operations assisting the military in Matabeleland at the time. Although the Commander of the Zimbabwe National Army at the time was General Mujuru and the Minister of State for Defense was Dr.

Sekeramayi, press reports indicate that General Mujuru and Dr. Sekeramayi were largely sidelined by Mnangagwa, who was the Minister of State for National Security in the President's Office, in the conduct of those operations. Press reports indicate that General Chiwenga, Air Chief Marshall Shiri, Shirihuru, Chipanga and Muzariri, among others, reported directly to Mnangagwa on a regular basis about the operations in Matabeleland. It appears from press reports that Mnangagwa was the co-ordinator of those military operations and that military and security commanders all reported to Mnangagwa. The operations resulted in atrocities, and there was an international outcry against the operation and demands for accountability by human rights groups. The fear of facing justice one day to account for those atrocities is what I think brought together Mnangagwa, Air Chief Marshall Perence Shiri and General Chiwenga; people like Shirihuru and Muzariri would have felt the same had they still been alive. I think that fear was also a strong motivation for the November 2017 military coup, to ensure that someone they did not trust to protect them once in power, like Dr. Sekeramayi, was prevented from assuming power.

I believe that Mnangagwa, Chiwenga, Shiri and other coup plotters were by the year 2017 convinced that Mugabe was about to hand over power because of poor health. Contrary to the disinformation peddled by the coup plotters, Mugabe was about to name his successor and that chosen successor had always been Dr. Sekeramayi, and was never Grace Mugabe, the President's wife. I believe the fear of the handover of power to Dr. Sekeramayi, who the coup plotters did not trust to protect them from accounting for the Matabeleland and other atrocities once in power, is what motivated the timing of the November 2017 coup.

The other influential person I met in 1998 was Dr. Ignatius Chombo, who was Minister of Higher and Tertiary Education. I knew from intelligence reports that Dr. Chombo was closely related to President Mugabe. I met him twice in his offices and went with him to lunch at an Italian restaurant at Avondale Shopping Centre in Harare. I discussed with him at length the network of officers that Mnangagwa continued to have in the CIO, and he was very attentive, but I was disappointed that instead of showing concern he at times seemed to express admiration for Mnangagwa's decisiveness and courage. His close relationship with President Mugabe was an opportunity for him to stop Mnangagwa's political manoeuvres through President Mugabe, but he appeared to be a fence-sitter. It is possible that Dr. Chombo deeply regretted this attitude when, according to press reports, he was held in military custody and severely assaulted by soldiers during the November 2017 military coup, shortly after he had been elevated by President Mugabe to the position of Minister of Finance.

ONE DAY IN October 1998 I received a telephone call from Dr. Tichaona Jokonya, who was Zimbabwe's ambassador to the United Nations Office in Geneva, Switzerland. I knew that Dr. Jokonya had President Mugabe's ear, since he would occasionally have dinner with the President and his family when he was in Harare. Dr. Jokonya was also related to Dr. Utete and Dr. Mariyawanda Nzuwa, chairman of the Public Service Commission, at the time. The three men, namely Utete, Jokonya and Nzuwa, had an overbearing influence on the Mugabe administration, which was made possible by Dr. Utete's closeness to the President. They all came from Chivhu but I never became close to any of them.

Dr. Jokonya told me that he had been closely following the media reports about the power struggle in the CIO between Chipanga and myself. He said he knew that we were only proxies and that the real battle was between Mnangagwa and General Mujuru. Dr. Jokonya told me that I should not expect Dr. Sekeramayi to intervene because he considered himself to be a "Mr. Clean" who avoided any controversy, because his calculations were that by not having a controversial image his chances of becoming President were higher. Dr. Jokonya said that this explained Dr. Sekeramayi's "chameleonic caution", which he displayed at all times. This was a reference to the indecisiveness Dr. Sekeramayi often displayed and his insistence on decision-making through consensus, even where there were ideological deep-seated differences which militated against reaching a consensus. For example, differences among top officers in the CIO arose from the fact that some were pro-Mnangagwa while others were pro-Mujuru, and differences on issues were usually centred on these differing political affiliations which could not be reconciled, yet Dr. Sekeramayi would insist on having a consensus among the officers in order for him to take decisions.

Dr. Jokonya advised me that the most appropriate person to meet with to discuss my problems with Chipanga was General Solomon Mujuru. The General was not only assertive in nature but he was also the kingmaker in the politics of Zimbabwe. Moreover, according to Dr. Jokonya, Mnangagwa considered the General to be his ultimate adversary in his presidential ambitions and respected him.

I may explain at this stage that my analysis of the contestants in the battle to succeed President Mugabe was as follows:

On the one side there was Mnangagwa, who was confident that he had the revolutionary credentials which qualified him to succeed President Mugabe. He had been in charge of security during the liberation war and during the period 1980 to 1988, when he was Minister of State for National Security in the President's Office. He had worked closely with Commanders of the Zimbabwe National Army and the Air Force of Zimbabwe during that period, and had created alliances with key figures in the CIO and the defense forces as a result. He was a qualified lawyer and so intellectually he also had suitable credentials. On the other side there was General Mujuru, who had equally impressive revolutionary credentials and connections. However, where the General fell short was that he did not have the academic credentials that Mnangagwa had. Moreover,

General Mujuru had a stuttering speech disability. He was aware of this, and that made him identify a candidate with academic credentials to run against Mnangagwa. He chose Dr. Sekeramayi, who also had liberation war credentials, was a qualified medical doctor and was very articulate; Dr. Sekeramayi was probably as articulate as President Mugabe was, and excellent at delivering public speeches. Thus, the contestants were Mnangagwa and Dr. Sekeramayi, but behind Dr. Sekeramayi there was General Mujuru, who had solid liberation war credentials and excellent connections in the military, made during the liberation war as deputy to the late General Josiah Magama Tongogara, and after independence while serving as the Commander of the Zimbabwe National Army.

I had not met General Mujuru on a one-on-one basis, and I sought advice from Dr. Jokonya about how to arrange to meet him. Dr. Jokonya advised that the best way would be to meet the General's wife, Mrs. Joyce Mujuru, and request her to arrange a meeting for me with the General.

I met Mrs. Mujuru a few weeks later in her office; she was a cabinet minister at the time. I briefed her about the power struggles in the CIO and quickly realized that she was aware of most of the issues, since they were in the public domain due to the incessant media publicity. Mrs. Mujuru felt that Dr. Sekeramayi should have intervened to resolve the matter, since it was obvious that Chipanga and I could not work together. She was also aware of the broader political battle behind the power struggle in the CIO. Mrs. Mujuru promised that she was going to discuss the matter with her husband, and would make an effort to arrange a meeting for me with General Mujuru. She took note of my direct line telephone number and told me to expect to hear from her or from General Mujuru.

I received a call in my office on my direct line a few days later from General Mujuru. He introduced himself to me on the phone as "Solomon", and told me that he had been informed by "Joyce" that I had important matters to discuss with him. General Mujuru was always informal and very down-to-earth in his approach. He invited me to come over to his offices in Milton Park in Harare.

I drove to the offices a few minutes later, and was quickly ushered into his office by a receptionist. I had interacted with the General several times over the years, during meetings attended by a lot of other people, and General Mujuru looked surprised to see me, saying that while my face was very familiar to him, he had not been familiar with my name. The General then suggested that we go for a drive and talk on the way. He appeared more comfortable discussing sensitive matters away from his office; I got the impression that he suspected his office may have been bugged. The General explained that he had bought a commercial building in Kuwadzana, a residential township west of Harare, and suggested that we drive there to inspect it. He asked that we use my official car, the one I had driven to his offices.

General Mujuru sat next to me in the passenger seat of my car as I drove to Kuwadzana. There were just the two of us in the car, but the General was receiving calls on his cellphone most of the time. He also made a few calls. One of the calls he made was to Maynard Muzariri who was Director of Counter-Intelligence in the CIO. The General had recently had his car stolen, while he was visiting some people in Cranborne suburb in Harare – a Toyota Landcruiser sport utility vehicle – and he demanded to know if Muzariri had recovered the stolen vehicle. When he got a negative reply, the General started to jokingly shout unprintable obscenities at Muzariri. Muzariri was widely known in the security sector to associate with criminal gangs, and those who knew this sought his help to recover property lost to thieves. Muzariri was known to have "influence" among criminal gangs, and so could arrange to recover property which had fallen into the hands of thieves. It appeared that General Mujuru had asked Muzariri to help him recover his stolen vehicle. I had discussed this matter with Dr. Sekeramayi and had expressed my concern that a CIO director could be allowed to associate with criminal gangs, but no action was ever taken against him.

Muzariri and John Kandeya, the Director Internal who succeeded Danny Stannard, were also known in the CIO to be openly pro- Mnangagwa. Muzariri often compared Mnangagwa with a "bulldog" and Dr. Sekeramayi with a "chihuahua", in terms of political clout and substance. Muzariri said quite openly in corridors in the CIO building that Mnangagwa had massive political influence while Dr. Sekeramayi had little or no political impact on the

Zimbabwe political scene. Chipanga had preferred either Muzariri or Kandeya to be appointed instead of me in the position of Deputy Director General, to help him drive the Mnangagwa political agenda. However, Kandeya died in 1997. He was replaced by Muzariri later, and Muzariri was later to become CIO Deputy Director General, until his death in 2011.

General Mujuru probably knew Muzariri from the liberation war days because Muzariri had been a senior member of the Zimbabwe African National Liberation Army (ZANLA). He had been a member of the ZANLA general staff, a level just below the level of High Command in seniority. Above the level of High Command there was only the level of Central Committee, which was the highest level of seniority in the ZANU hierarchy during the liberation war. Whether Mujuru knew that Muzariri had strong political affiliations to Mnangagwa or not, I was not able to ascertain.

Apart from his chat with Muzariri, General Mujuru also had a chat with Tirivanhu Mudariki and his wife. Mudariki was a member of Parliament at the time and was close to the General. The General also jokingly shouted obscenities at both of them.

General Mujuru then switched off his cellphone and asked me to brief him about why I had come to meet him. I briefed him about all the problems I was having in the CIO with Chipanga, and explained to him that Dr. Sekeramayi had so far not intervened. The General indicated that he was aware that Chipanga was pushing Mnangagwa's political agenda in the CIO. The General said that he was the only person who could keep Mnangagwa in check about his political ambitions. He thanked me for the brief and promised he would use his influence to ensure that a solution was found to the problems I was having with Chipanga. After the General had inspected the building in Kuwadzana, we drove back to Milton Park and I dropped him off at his offices.

I knew that General Mujuru and Dr. Sekeramayi were very close and were probably even related. For example, I had seen them together at the funeral of the father of Edmund Garwe, who was Governor and Resident Minister for Mashonaland East Province at the time. As the most senior member of the province, the General had been asked to deliver the eulogy on behalf of ZANU (P.F.) but, aware of his speech disability, the General had asked Dr. Sekeramayi to deliver the eulogy on his behalf. The General and Dr. Sekeramayi spent a lot of time together on social occasions during weekends, and I knew that the General had a big influence over him.

After our meeting, I was very hopeful that General Mujuru would lean on Dr. Sekeramayi and ensure that a solution was found to the problems I was having in my working relationship with Chipanga.

A few weeks later, rumours started circulating to the effect that two senior army officers were being considered for appointment to senior positions in the CIO. Meanwhile, matters had come to a head in the CIO with regards to my working relationship with Chipanga. In late October 1998, Dr. Sekeramayi approved Chipanga's recommendation to set up a CIO team to investigate allegations of corruption against me, relating to the real estate investments that I had initiated during my time as Director of Administration. Muzariri was appointed head of the investigating team.

This development shocked me for two reasons. Firstly, I had recently met General Mujuru, who had given me the impression that he understood the political context behind the hostility that Chipanga was displaying toward me. The setting up of an investigating team targeting me did not appear to be consistent with the impression that the General had created in me. Secondly, I considered it unprocedural for a team of CIO officers junior to me to investigate me. Moreover, Muzariri was semi-literate and did not have the capacity to comprehend the mechanics and objectives of the investment initiatives that I had undertaken. I could not understand how Dr. Sekeramayi had been persuaded to accept this course of action. I felt Chipanga and the pro-Mnangagwa network in the CIO were prevailing and had won over Dr. Sekeramayi to their side, in spite of all my efforts to make influential people like General Mujuru appreciate the nature of the political battle at play.

In November 1998, Chipanga and I were both summoned to Dr. Sekeramayi's office one afternoon. Dr Sekeramayi handed to each of us a letter of dismissal from the CIO signed by President Mugabe. The letters indicated that we were being dismissed because we had been unable to work together. That development ended my career in the CIO.

I soon became aware that two brigadiers from the Zimbabwe National Army, who had absolutely no background in intelligence matters, had been appointed by President Mugabe on the recommendation of Dr. Sekeramayi to the positions of Director General and Deputy Director General. Brigadier Elisha Muzonzini was appointed Director General, replacing Chipanga, and Brigadier Happyton Bonyongwe was appointed Deputy Director General, replacing me. Both appointments were with immediate effect. Muzonzini was reassigned a few years later to the Ministry of Foreign Affairs, and Bonyongwe then took over as CIO Director General until the year 2017 (he was appointed Minister of Justice by Mugabe, and lasted just a few weeks in that position before the November 2017 coup), when President Mugabe was overthrown by Mnangagwa in the military coup.

Many people in the CIO were astounded by these appointments. They wondered how two people from outside the organization could be appointed to the two most senior positions in the CIO. It soon became public knowledge in the CIO and outside the organization that the two brigadiers were friends with General Mujuru. They were appointed because of that friendship after the General had persuaded Dr. Sekeramayi to recommend to President Mugabe their appointment. The appointments were thus motivated by corruption and not merit.

I felt that I had been let down not just by General Mujuru, but by Dr. Sekeramayi and President Mugabe as well. I felt that the three were all underestimating the political threat they were facing at the hands of the Mnangagwa faction. The General should not have put his personal interests ahead of political and national interests. General Mujuru was to be reported by the media subsequently boasting that he was now in control of the CIO because Muzonzini and Bonyongwe, his protégés, were now in charge of it.

The fact of the matter, however, was that Muzonzini and Bonyongwe would just be figure-heads presiding ineffectively over an organization which was pro-Mnangagwa through and through. As people who had come from outside, it would take them a long time to understand the power-play and intricate web of alliances in the organization. The Mnangagwa network in the CIO would be determined to neutralize them or to subtly win them over to their side. For example, the pro-Mnangagwa network in the CIO, from the time Chipanga was CIO Director General, included Isaac Moyo, who Chipanga recommended in the 1990s for a diplomatic post in the Embassy of Zimbabwe in South Africa, as First Secretary. Chipanga and Moyo were very close on account of the fact that they both belonged to the Mnangagwa faction. Moyo was to be seconded to a diplomatic post in Addis Ababa after Bonyongwe had become CIO Director General, in spite of that background. In the year 2013, Moyo was seconded by Bonyongwe from the CIO to the Ministry of Foreign Affairs, as ambassador to South Africa. It was as if

Bonyongwe did not know the fact that Moyo was close to Mnangagwa. Indeed, soon after overthrowing President Mugabe in November 2017, Mnangagwa appointed Isaac Moyo to be CIO Director General. Thus Bonyongwe, who had been Mujuru's trusted protégé, had all along elevated Mnangagwa's trusted political ally.

Whereas General Mujuru felt secure and lost guard in the mistaken belief that Muzonzini and Bonyongwe, who were supposedly loyal to him, were now in control of the CIO, all indications are that this was a huge and costly miscalculation on the part of the General – a miscalculation which may even have ultimately cost the General's life in August 2011. The General died in very suspicious circumstances when he was burnt to death in his house in Beatrice, forty kilometres south of Harare. It is difficult to understand how the CIO failed to prevent that death, if the organization's leadership was as loyal to him and competent as the General claimed.

PART

THREE

THE POST-CIO SERVICE PERIOD

ALTHOUGH CHIPANGA LEFT the CIO at the same time that I left the organization in November 1998, he continued to influence events and developments in the CIO, through the pro-Mnangagwa network which was still more or less intact. Accordingly, the investigations against me by the CIO team headed by Muzariri continued. I started hearing that some senior officials in the Commercial Bank of Zimbabwe (CBZ) were working with the CIO in an attempt to obtain information of a criminal nature against me. Apparently, some members of the senior staff at the CBZ were part of the pro-Mnangagwa network. Mnangagwa's network included not only members of the judiciary, legal practitioners, government officials and others, but bankers as well.

The background to the involvement of the CBZ was that a few months after my appointment as Director of Administration in 1993, I discussed with the Director General of the CIO Dr. Mashingaidze what I felt was the need to transfer CIO's banking accounts from Barclays Bank to CBZ. Since the colonial period, the CIO maintained banking accounts at Barclays Bank; I felt there was exposure of CIO's financial status if the organization maintained these accounts with Barclays. A number of senior CIO officers who had left the organization were known to officials in the bank and I was worried that if client confidentiality was breached by the bank then the CIO's financial situation could be compromised. Dr. Mashingaidze agreed with me on the need to move the accounts from Barclays Bank. The Bank of Credit and Commerce, which had run into a financial crisis, had just been reconstituted by the government into the Commercial Bank of Zimbabwe (CBZ), and Gideon Gono had been appointed to head the new bank. That was before he was appointed governor of the Reserve Bank of Zimbabwe. I met Gideon Gono at his office and briefed him about the need to move the CIO bank accounts from Barclays Bank to CBZ, asking him to ensure that his officers maintained strict client confidentiality with regard to the bank accounts. I also requested him to approve an overdraft facility for the CIO, which the CIO could use if Treasury granted its approval. There were cash flow problems at the time in government, and I did not want to face the prospect of CIO officers failing to get paid their salaries, but I was also aware that an overdraft facility was a loan and only the Minister of Finance could obtain loans for government. The meeting with Gono went very well, but I got worried subsequently when I started hearing that some senior CBZ officials were close and loyal to Mnangagwa. Mnangagwa had acted as Minister of Finance a number of times and I thought this explained the reported close working relations between them, but some reports even went further to express concern about the fact that President Mugabe had entrusted his personal banking to CBZ senior staff, yet Mnangagwa was very influential among the CBZ leadership.

The investigations against me by the CIO culminated in my arrest one Friday morning in March 1999, by the Criminal Investigations Department's (C.I.D.) Fraud Squad, which fell under the police. A blue, dilapidated

Land Rover vehicle drove up to my house in Borrowdale Brooke, Harare that Friday morning and three C.I.D. officers alighted from the vehicle and asked me to get in. They produced police identity cards and told me that I was under arrest. I had planned to travel with my family later that day to Mutare in eastern Zimbabwe, to spend the weekend with my in-laws, and my wife Sibongile Mukandi was at work at CABS (Central Africa Building Society) at the time. She worked in the money market department and her job was very demanding. Moreover, she was seven months pregnant at the time. My arrest would really put her under enormous pressure.

The police were in the habit of making arrests on Fridays, so that the person arrested spent the weekend in police custody without the police having to take them to court in forty-eight hours, as required by law; this was because weekends were not counted in computing the forty-eight hours. The police also tended to succumb to pressure exerted by influential complainants to apply undue pressure on the person arrested, and in this case Muzariri, through his connections in the C.I.D. and the police hierarchy, was applying pressure to make my time in police custody very uncomfortable.

Muzariri's rural home was in Mount Darwin, about one hundred and sixty kilometres north of Harare, and he was close to Police Commissioner General Augustine Chihuri, as they both came from the same general home area in Mashonaland Central Province. This acquaintance was to prove costly to me in the following months, with the CIO abusing their influence with the police to victimize me. The situation was made worse by the fact that Chihuri and Happyton Bonyongwe became close friends after Bonyongwe became CIO Director General, after taking over from Elisha Muzonzini in the year 2000. The persecution against me that occurred over the next decade was made possible by that friendship, as the police readily complied with every request from the CIO to victimize me without regard to whether the request was legal or not.

I was taken that Friday morning to Morris Police Depot in Harare and interrogated the whole day by the police's C.I.D. Fraud Squad. The head of the police investigating team, Superintendent Ernest Kangara, however, admitted to me afterwards that the interrogation had not yielded the incriminating evidence that they had hoped to find, but added that the police were under immense pressure from the CIO to charge me. They were going to do so, and it would be up to the court to determine whether a crime had been committed.

Towards sunset that Friday I was taken to Borrowdale Police Station in Harare and locked up in police cells for the weekend. The cell was filthy and the conditions absolutely inhumane. The blankets were infested with lice and I got a nasty spider bite wound on my arm, which bothered me for weeks afterwards. There was an intense foul smell in the cell from the excrement in the overflowing toilet, which I and four or five other accused persons sat around day and night. My wife and her parents brought me food the whole weekend and that was a huge relief, because the food provided in the cells was highly unpalatable. My lawyer Aston Musunga had been out of Harare when I was arrested on Friday, but he was back in town on Saturday and interviewed me that weekend. He assured me that I would get bail soon after the weekend.

My arrest and detention in police custody were given extensive press coverage which was highly defamatory of me. The media coverage was driven by the journalists who had all along been taking orders from the CIO, in pursuance of the pro-Mnangagwa political agenda.

On the Monday following the unpleasant weekend, I and two other accused persons were taken to court and charged with contravening a section of the Prevention of Corruption Act or, alternatively, fraud. A magistrate remanded us out of custody on bail, to a date in June 1999.

In June 1999 the matter was further remanded to September, and in September the matter was again further remanded to December 1999. All this postponement was because the police investigations had not produced evidence constituting a *prima facie* case which could be taken to trial.

Meanwhile, in May 1999 the police impounded my personal pickup truck, a Mazda B2500 DX, which had a canopy and other extras and was almost brand new. The police said they would produce the vehicle in court as an exhibit during my trial. There was never a trial but I never saw the vehicle again. Contrary to the claims by the police that the vehicle was impounded to be used as an exhibit, sources in the police told my lawyers that the vehicle was used on personal errands by a few senior police and CIO officers, soon after being impounded. The errands included night hunting expeditions by Muzariri and Chihuri in game parks. The vehicle continued to be used in that manner until it became a wreck. No explanation was ever provided by the police about the fate of that vehicle. This was a clear manifestation of the brazen abuse of office by the police and CIO under Chihuri and Bonyongwe respectively, and it appeared that the two State institutions had become a law unto themselves during the late stages of President Mugabe's rule.

At my remand hearing on 31st January 2000, my lawyers and the lawyers for my co-accused applied to the court that we be removed from remand because the police investigations had gone on for too long without yielding any evidence which could enable the State to take us to trial. The police had repeatedly asked for postponements of the matter because they were not ready for trial. The presiding magistrate granted the application and criticized the police for arresting us in order to start investigations, when the law requires the police to make an arrest only after investigations have yielded sufficient evidence to constitute a *prima facie* case against an accused person. The court removed me and my co-accused from remand, told us we were now free persons and ruled that if the State wished to pursue the matter in the future the prosecution would have to proceed by way of summons against us. It was not legally competent for the police to arrest us again in connection with the same matter, the court ruled.

The officers in the CIO who had been pushing for my prosecution were so angered by this outcome that Muzariri, in his foolishness, was seen tearing up a print newspaper that had reported my removal from remand by the court. It was as if that was the single newspaper that had been printed and that tearing it up would prevent the public from reading about my removal from remand. To people like him, it did not matter what the law said, all they cared about was that I should be victimized because my political affiliation differed from theirs.

IN JUNE 2000 I received a letter signed by Dr. Sekeramayi, who was still the Minister of State for National Security in the President's Office. The letter advised me that the Cabinet had decided I should be retired from the CIO on full pension benefits, following my removal from remand by the court on 31st January 2000, since that meant that there were no allegations of a criminal nature I was facing anymore. The letter advised me that my pension benefits would soon be processed and that I should expect payment of those benefits to me in due course. In a perfect world I would have expected my removal from remand to persuade Minister Sekeramayi and President Mugabe to consider my reinstatement in the CIO, but I was nevertheless relieved that I was going to be retired on full pension benefits.

When I waited for weeks without receiving the pension benefits, I started to hear from the grapevine that the pro-Mnangagwa network in the CIO was resisting the Cabinet directive to process my pension benefits, and had sat on my CIO personal file instead of making it available to the Pensions Office for my pension to be processed.

Meanwhile, there had been a cabinet reshuffle after June 2000 and the CIO was now headed by a new minister. The Minister of State for National Security in the President's Office was now Nicholas Goche. I expected that Goche would have been briefed about the matter of the processing of my pension benefits on taking over from Dr. Sekeramayi.

A colleague and sympathizer in the CIO told me that my pension was unlikely to be processed in spite of the Cabinet directive because of resistance in the CIO, unless I approached someone of influence to push for the processing of the pension. The colleague introduced me to a prison warden at Manyame Prison, near the Robert Gabriel International Airport in Harare. It sounded improbable to me that a prison warden could facilitate the processing of my pension, but it turned out that the particular warden I was introduced to could! The prison warden was a close relative of Mnangagwa, who had been appointed Speaker of Parliament by President Mugabe after failing to win a seat in parliamentary elections of the year 2000, thus making it difficult for him to be appointed a cabinet minister. The colleague advised me to explain to the warden the problem regarding the processing of my pension. He told me that the warden could approach Mnangagwa on my behalf and ask Mnangagwa to use his influence with the CIO to get my pension processed. I hesitated, but on reflection decided to follow the colleague's advice.

After meeting the prison warden a few times I presented my problem regarding the processing of my pension to him and asked him to approach Mnangagwa about the matter on my behalf. He agreed to help and a few weeks later, in November 2000, the warden told me he had good news for me. He told me that Mnangagwa had agreed to intercede in the matter on my behalf informally, and had requested Minister Goche to push the CIO to release my personal file and forward it to the Pensions Office, so that my pension could be processed. Goche had immediately done so and my pension had been processed the previous week. The warden then told me the exact amount that I would receive in December 2000 by way of pension commutation as a lump sum, and how much the monthly payments I would receive after that would be.

For once I felt indebted to Mnangagwa, because it turned out that the amounts that I received in December 2000 were exactly what the prison warden had told me they would be. I was not able to guess why Mnangagwa had agreed to help, however. The Cabinet directive that approved my pension had been made while Mnangagwa was still sitting in Cabinet and so he had personal knowledge of it. He must have thought it an act of indiscretion for his people in the CIO to flagrantly ignore that directive by resisting the processing of my pension. He probably wanted to avoid an open collision course that exposed his divergent political agenda to President Mugabe. I appreciated Mnangagwa's help but it did not escape my attention that the implications of this episode were grave; Mnangagwa had demonstrated that he could give orders to cabinet ministers to do certain things. This was clear evidence of the magnitude of State capture by Mnangagwa during President Mugabe's era.

OVER THE NEXT few weeks, in January 2001, I had the uneasy sense that my family and I were being followed. We went to my rural home in Chivhu a few times and to my wife's home in Mutare, and each time we travelled we noticed that there were one or two vehicles which kept a discreet distance behind us all the way. My family comprised my wife Sibongile; two daughters Lisa and Kundisai, who were nine and two years old respectively; two daughters and a son from my previous marriage, namely Tamara and Tanaka, who were eighteen and eleven years old respectively; and Bryan, who was twenty-one years old at the time and was studying medicine at the University of Zimbabwe. We also lived with my wife's younger sister Rufaro Chikwanda, who was fifteen years old at the time and went to Vainona High School in Harare. Tamara went to Dominican Convent High School, while Tanaka and Lisa went to Borrowdale Primary School, all in Harare.

My wife and I discussed our fears and decided that it was time we left Zimbabwe for the sake of our lives. Our enemies in the CIO had reached a dead-end trying to send me to jail through a spurious prosecution which had been thrown out by the court, and it appeared that they were now considering eliminating me. We applied to several overseas universities to be enrolled for university study, and in May 2001 our applications for undergraduate study were accepted by Saint Mary's University in Halifax, Canada. My wife had a Bachelor of Business Studies degree from the University of Zimbabwe. I had Bachelor of Law (B.L.) and Bachelor of Laws (LLB) degrees, also from the University of Zimbabwe. We were both admitted in the Bachelor of Commerce program at Saint Mary's University.

We applied at the Canadian High Commission in Harare, in May 2001, for study permits for the family. We decided that we should not disturb Bryan's studies in medical school at the University of Zimbabwe and so he was to remain behind. He would be living with his mother in the matrimonial home in Avondale, Harare. Title in the home had been transferred from me to his mother as part of the divorce settlement. Everyone else – namely my wife Sibongile, Tamara, Tanaka, Lisa, Rufaro and I – applied for study permits and we applied for a visitor's permit for Kundisai, who was not yet in school. We went through very intense medical tests as part of the application process and obtained police clearance certificates from police offices at Morris Depot in Harare, which were a declaration that none of us was facing criminal charges in Zimbabwe. All of these documents were required by the Canadian High

Commission in order for them to consider issuing the permits we had applied for.

Zimbabwe was to leave the Commonwealth Organization in 2003, after President Mugabe's government was subjected to severe criticism for committing human rights abuses. President Mugabe was to decide to withdraw Zimbabwe's membership from the Commonwealth rather than implement governance reforms which were in compliance with the Commonwealth's governance standards. This was a very selfish decision, which deprived many Zimbabweans of opportunities for scholarships and other benefits which came from membership of the Commonwealth. Fortunately, the Canadian High Commission still maintained an office in Harare in 2001, and so we were able to submit our applications for study permits at the Canadian High Commission offices in Harare. The offices were later to be relocated to Pretoria in South Africa.

We were informed by the Canadian High Commission that our study permits would be ready by the end of July 2001, and we accordingly bought plane tickets for departure from Zimbabwe on 31st July 2001. There were delays in the issuing of the study permits, however, and those delays caused a lot of anxiety and sleepless nights for my family. We had in the meantime sold our Borrowdale family home very reluctantly. In view of the experience we'd had regarding the impounding of our pickup truck in 1999, and its misuse and permanent disappearance at the hands of the police and CIO, we felt our home was at risk if we rented it out; the police and CIO could similarly abuse their authority and unlawfully transfer title in the house from us to themselves. And so we decided to sell the house and apply the proceeds to starting a new life in Canada for ourselves.

On 31st July 2001, my wife, Rufaro, and children went to the Canadian High Commission offices to enquire about the permits, while I took all our luggage to the airport. It was a very difficult day for us, because we were on edge due to the uncertainty surrounding the issuing of the study permits. Our flight from Harare was scheduled to depart Harare at three p.m., but as of midday we still did not have the study permits. The permits were eventually issued around one p.m., to our immense relief, and my wife and family then sped to the airport, where we quickly checked ourselves in for the flight to Johannesburg, South Africa. The British Airways flight left Harare on schedule and we thanked God that we had made it. There was on the flight my wife, Lisa, Kundisai, Tamara, Tanaka, Rufaro and myself.

Just over an hour later the seven of us were in Johannesburg, South Africa, where we took a connecting Air France flight that evening and landed in Paris, France the following morning. We proceeded to Heathrow Airport in London later that day. After a stopover for a few hours, we took an Air Canada flight and landed in Halifax, on Canada's east coast, on 1st August 2001.

We had been allocated university accommodation on campus at Saint Mary's University, as part of the process of applying for admission to the university, and our apartment was on the twenty- first floor. It was a two-bedroomed apartment which was to be the home for the seven of us for the next four-and-a-half years. My wife and I shared one bedroom with Kundisai while the other four girls occupied the other bedroom. We were cramped in that apartment, but happy to be alive and in Canada.

There was to be a hurricane which hit Halifax a year later and we were terrified on the twenty-first floor, as the high-rise building appeared to swing from side to side because of the strong winds. We were, however, immensely relieved that we were in Canada together as a family, making an effort to start a new life.

MEANWHILE, BACK IN Zimbabwe Chipanga and Pearson Mbalekwa had become members of Parliament. Mbalekwa was the nephew of Mnangagwa, who had a few years earlier been posted to the Zimbabwe Embassy in Nairobi, Kenya by Chipanga, while the latter was still Director of External Operations in the CIO. Mnangagwa had used his political influence to have the two elected as members of Parliament.

The two M.P.s soon started to claim in Parliament that I had fled Zimbabwe to escape criminal charges I was facing. They abused their parliamentary immunity and privileges, and used the platform of Parliament to regularly raise questions directed at the Minister of Justice, demanding to know what the Minister was doing to ensure that I was brought back to Zimbabwe to face justice. They claimed that I was a fugitive from justice and they used their contacts in the Zimbabwe media to have the parliamentary debates about me publicized in the print media. They made some very inflammatory and defamatory claims against me, falsely claiming that I had been scheduled to appear in court for a remand hearing in the year 2000, but had instead fled from Zimbabwe on the day of that remand hearing. All of this was very elaborately choreographed. The Minister of Justice, to whom the questions were directed in Parliament, was Patrick Chinamasa at the time, who was very close to Mnangagwa, and was to be appointed Minister of Finance by Mnangagwa after his overthrow of President Mugabe in November 2017. Chinamasa deliberately avoided dismissing these questions even though he knew they had no basis, because it was a plot to have these questions raised in Parliament over and over again, to ensure maximum publicity.

Mbalekwa and Chipanga were to spend the next four or five years regularly making these defamatory statements in Parliament against me. They pretended that their motivation was to ensure that the administration of justice took place equally, fairly and without impunity. They never hinted at the nature of their connections to Mnangagwa, nor the political battles they were waging with and for Mnangagwa against perceived political opponents like myself. At the time I mistakenly dismissed these incessant attacks which were taking place in Parliament and in the

Zimbabwe media against me as inconsequential. I did not fully realize the determination that Chipanga, Mbalekwa and the pro-Mnangagwa network in the CIO had to relentlessly pursue me as their political opponent.

My wife and I pursued our studies at Saint Mary's University under extremely difficult circumstances until my wife had to cut short her studies when our funds ran out, and took up full-time employment. The entire family depended on her for upkeep for years afterwards. She later completed her studies through private study on a part-time basis, until she qualified to become a Chartered Professional Accountant (CPA) of Canada. I pursued my studies, which were very challenging, because I had crossed over from Law, which I studied at the University of Zimbabwe, to Economics, and I had to work hard on Mathematics, which is very prominent in Economics. The other challenge was that I did not have a computer background yet most of the studies at Saint Mary's University revolved around the use of computers. I had to quickly learn to use computers in basic and sophisticated tasks, including graphing techniques and statistical computations, using computer software like Stata.

I took up odd jobs on campus to supplement the family income. We made a living that way until I graduated at Saint Mary's University in Spring 2005, with a joint Bachelor of Arts Honours degree in Economics and a Bachelor of Commerce *(magna cum laude)* degree majoring in Finance, and was inducted in the Hall of Fame of the President of Saint Mary's University in 2005.

In August 2005 we moved to Ottawa, Canada's capital, where I graduated with a Master of Arts degree in Economics in 2006 from Carleton University. The family then moved in 2007 to Toronto, where my wife had been transferred to. She continued to be the family breadwinner. I took on a few odd jobs in Toronto until I became employed on a full-time basis as a Senior Business Analyst at Rogers Communications Incorporated, a major Canadian telecommunications company.

Meanwhile, we had applied to renew our study permits in 2003 but the whole family had not received a response from the Canadian immigration authorities. As a result, the whole family was without valid Canadian immigration papers from 2004. We made enquiries at various immigration offices in Halifax and Ottawa, but all we were told was that the applications for the extension of our permits were being considered.

In January 2007 we decided to apply for refugee status in Canada as a family, as we continued to read reports in the online Zimbabwe media that I was regarded as a fugitive from justice by the Zimbabwe government. We lodged our application for refugee status in Toronto, Canada in January 2007, and were advised that we would receive a response in due course.

Sometime in early 2008 I received a letter from Canadian immigration authorities, inviting me to attend a hearing in connection with the application by my family for refugee status in Canada. I attended the hearing one morning and the presiding officer informed me that, after going through my application papers, Canadian immigration authorities had noticed that I had been a senior official in President Mugabe's government. He added that the Canadian government considered the Mugabe government a rogue regime in that it had committed gross human rights violations over the years and had also committed crimes against humanity. The presiding officer informed me that since I had served the Mugabe government in a senior capacity and in the CIO, the Canadian government regarded me as complicit in crimes against humanity, even though there was no evidence that I had personally or directly been involved in committing any such crimes.

The presiding officer explained that, accordingly, Canadian immigration authorities had decided to separate my application for refugee status from the applications by the rest of my family, since they had not been in the Mugabe government and were therefore not complicit in the crimes committed by the Mugabe regime. The applications by members of my family would be considered at a hearing in due course, but my application would not be considered at that hearing. Instead, since the Canadian government detested the Mugabe government and I had been associated with it, Canadian immigration authorities would soon commence a process leading to my deportation from Canada.

The legal process leading up to my deportation from Canada was a lengthy one and involved a number of hearings. It was very traumatic to me and my family knowing that the process would likely end in my enforced separation from my family, if I was sent back to Zimbabwe. I was also aware that elements in the CIO linked to Mnangagwa were still after me. I had explained in great detail in my application for refugee status that I had been pursued and persecuted for political reasons in Zimbabwe, by elements in the Zimbabwe government led by Mnangagwa, who was still in the top leadership of the Zimbabwe government. I explained that my life and liberty would be threatened if I was sent back to Zimbabwe.

In spite of my protestations, the Canadian immigration authorities continued to pursue the process aimed at my deportation from Canada. A deportation order was served on me in the year 2010 and in spite of my efforts to fight it in the Canadian immigration hierarchy and in the courts through lawyers, the deportation order was confirmed and I was set to be deported from Canada on 21st September 2011.

Before being deported I attended a hearing with my family in July 2011, where I spent the greater part of a day explaining to Canadian immigration authorities why members of my family feared for their lives if they were sent back to Zimbabwe. I explained that their fears were reasonable and justified because they were connected to me and, since I was being persecuted by members of the Zimbabwe government, members of my family were at risk if they were sent back to Zimbabwe. This argument was accepted by the presiding judge and a few months after that hearing all the members of my family were granted refugee status in Canada. They were later granted permanent residence in Canada, and subsequently Canadian citizenship.

A month prior to my deportation I was advised that Canadian immigration authorities had formed the impression that I was law- abiding, so there would be no need to send me to an immigration detention centre pending my physical removal from Canada. I was to be allowed to continue to live at home with my family until my deportation, but I was required to report to an immigration officer twice a week until my removal from Canada. I was also informed that a one-way plane ticket had been purchased for me and I would be departing Pearson International Airport near Toronto for Washington DC on 21st September 2011. I would take an overnight connecting flight to Addis Ababa, Ethiopia the same day, then take a connecting flight to Harare, Zimbabwe the following day. I was also advised that for the entire duration of the flight from Toronto to Harare I would technically be under arrest – although I would not be in handcuffs – and two officials from the Canada Border Services Agency would escort me all the way and hand me over to Zimbabwe immigration authorities at the airport in Harare.

This was a most traumatic period for me and my family. I was in full-time employment at the time as a Senior Business Analyst and earned a good bi-weekly salary. My wife and I had entered into a rent-to-buy agreement to purchase the home in Oakville, Ontario that we were living in. We had paid a substantial deposit and had a monthly financial commitment in terms of the rent-to-buy agreement. My deportation meant that I had to give up my job and the salary that came with it. Since my wife could not afford to continue paying the monthly instalments to buy the home on her own, my deportation also meant reneging on the rent-to-buy agreement and forfeiting all the money we had paid in terms of the agreement. My deportation from Canada was therefore at considerable financial and emotional cost to my family.

During the evening on 20th September 2011 my wife packed a suitcase for me, the one suitcase that I was allowed on the flight to Harare. I was required to be at Pearson International Airport by three a.m. on 21st September 2011. We could not get any sleep at all as a family on the night of 20th September, because we were all very anxious and traumatized. My youngest daughter Kundisai, who was twelve years old at the time, was too young to comprehend what was happening. She went to bed a few hours before my departure for the airport. It tore my heart to pieces when I got into her bedroom to bid her farewell a few hours later. She looked dazed and went back to sleep in a state of confusion. My wife drove me to the airport accompanied by our daughter Lisa and my wife's sister Rufaro.

We found the two officers from the Canada Border Services Agency waiting for me when we got to the airport at three a.m. on 21st September 2011. Lisa cried out loud as we bid farewell. She had been at work earlier that night at Starbucks, where she had a part-time job. Rufaro looked devastated. My wife Sibongile is a very brave woman; I could tell that she was devastated but she remained strong enough to drive Lisa and Rufaro back home after we bid farewell. At that point, we didn't know if or when we would ever see each other again.

I was quickly taken to the check-in counters by the Canada Border Services Agency officials. The airport was virtually deserted at that early morning hour. An hour or two later I was taken to a small, ten-seater aircraft which flew us to Washington DC. I kept exchanging SMS messages via my phone with Tanaka, who was at the University of Ottawa. She was devastated but I kept reassuring her that all would be well in the end. Tamara had equally been devastated, and had raised money for us to pay lawyers to fight the deportation, but all of that had been in vain.

The Canada Border Services Agency officials kept a close eye on me during the flight, but did not use the handcuffs that I quickly saw they had. We arrived in Washington DC early in the morning, and a few hours later took a connecting Ethiopian Airways overnight flight to Addis Ababa. On the morning of 22nd September 2011 we took another Ethiopian Airways connecting flight and landed at Harare International Airport (later renamed Robert Gabriel Mugabe Airport) around one p.m. I was back in Zimbabwe.

The two Canada Border Services Agency officials disembarked from the plane and walked with me into the arrivals hall at the airport. I immediately saw a large group of people in the hall and it was obvious that they were expecting me. My travel document had been issued by the Zimbabwe Embassy in Ottawa, specifically for my return to Zimbabwe. I could see that there was communication in an agitated manner between the Zimbabwe authorities who were in the arrivals hall at the airport and the two Canada Border Services Agency officers, who immediately handed me over to the Zimbabwe immigration authorities.

I was promptly handcuffed and told by an officer that I was under arrest. There were many journalists, CIO and police Criminal Investigations Department (CID) officers in the hall. I could see that the two Canada Border Services Agency officials looked satisfied and excited as I was handcuffed. Clearly, my arrest upon arrival in Harare had been discussed with them by Zimbabwean authorities and was anticipated by them. The two Canadian officials walked away in the company of Zimbabwean authorities after I had been arrested, their task having been accomplished.

Journalists took pictures of me and called me a fugitive from justice. They asked me why I had fled from Zimbabwe years back and if I thought that justice would not catch up with me ultimately. I declined to answer their questions. I realized that arrangements had been made by Zimbabwean authorities to give maximum publicity to my enforced return to and arrival in Zimbabwe, and my arrest.

My wife and I had advised relatives in Zimbabwe that I was being deported from Canada and was scheduled to arrive in Harare on 22nd September 2011, and my wife's parents and my wife's cousin were at the airport to meet me. However, due to the elaborate arrangements that had been made for my arrest upon arrival, they were prevented from meeting me; it was only hours later that they were allowed to, briefly. I was instead taken away by the CID to a police station a few metres away from the main airport building, where a group of CID officers started to interrogate me.

A more senior CID officer arrived a few hours later and took me to his official car, which then drove into Harare. I was made to sit between two CID officers on the back seat of the car and there were two more CID officers in the front seats. Before departing the airport I demanded to be allowed to meet my in-laws, who I knew were at the airport. The officers grudgingly allowed me to meet them. I briefly met my in-laws and my wife's cousin, who asked the CID officers where they were taking me to. They were told that I was being taken to Ahmed House, the CID Fraud Squad headquarters in central Harare, for questioning. I asked my wife's cousin to contact my lawyer Aston Musunga, and to inform him that I needed his help, as I was under arrest.

In the car on the way to Ahmed House I asked the senior CID officer why I was under arrest. He told me that the CID had a warrant for my arrest, which had been issued by a magistrate. I asked to see the warrant and the officer gave it to me to examine. I immediately realized that the warrant of arrest was fake. It was fake because the warrant falsely claimed that I had failed to appear in court for a remand hearing on 31st January 2000. In fact, I and my co-accused had not only appeared in court on 31st January 2000, but on that day our lawyers had applied for our removal from remand and the court had granted the application. The court had ruled on that day that the police had taken too long to conduct their investigations and the investigations had failed to yield any evidence to enable the prosecution to proceed to trial. Consequently, the court on 31st January 2000 removed me and my co-accused from remand and ordered that we should be set free. If the State wished to pursue the matter in the future, then it should proceed by way of summons, but we could not be arrested again in connection with the same charges, the court had ordered on 31st January 2000.

The current CID team was a new one; there was not a single officer in the car with me who had been part of the original investigating team in 1999, when I was arrested and charged. I could sense that the members of the new CID investigating team genuinely believed in the validity of the warrant of arrest. They were not aware that, in fact, on 31st January 2000 I and my co- accused had been removed from remand and had not failed to appear in court, as was being claimed in the warrant of arrest.

That afternoon at Ahmed House I explained to the CID officers how defective the warrant of arrest was and they went into panic mode, realizing they may have made an unlawful arrest. Numerous telephone calls were made to police headquarters and I could clearly tell that the

CID officers had become anxious and uncomfortable. Meanwhile, my lawyer Aston Musunga had indicated that he had other commitments and could not attend to me. This was a blow to me, because he was the lawyer who had represented me in court on 31st January 2000, and so had personal knowledge of the fact that I had attended court on that day, and had been removed from remand by the court. Instead, he sent a junior lawyer who interviewed me, but it was obvious to me that he lacked the ability and experience to competently handle my defense. My in-laws and cousin in the meantime came to Ahmed House and took away my luggage for safekeeping. They advised me that they would remain in Harare to monitor the situation until the matter was finalized. My in-laws lived in Mutare in eastern Zimbabwe.

This was Thursday 22nd September 2011. That evening I was taken to Harare Central Police Station and locked up for the night in police cells. I had never experienced such horror before. I remembered my difficult experience in the police cells at Borrowdale Police Station back in March 1999, but the conditions in the cells at Harare Central Police Station were much worse. It was overcrowded in the cells and there were lice all over the thin and worn blankets. We were meant to spend the night sitting and not laying down, and whenever I started to doze off a police officer would suddenly open the heavy steel door and order us to stand up and get ready for a head count. This took place throughout the night. I could not understand why the police feared anyone could escape from the cells under such tight security. It was a night during which everyone in the cells was subjected to extreme harassment by the police and it was a very traumatic experience.

The CID officers had told me that I would be taken out of the cells early in the morning on Friday 23rd September, in order to be taken to court. In the morning that Friday I kept hoping and expecting my name to be called out whenever the door was opened by police officers, who were taking people to court, but no one came until almost midday.

I was taken back to Ahmed House around midday and I spent a few hours there, just sitting in a chair. I had last eaten the previous day just before I was taken to the cells, so my wife's cousin brought me food from a retail food outlet and I was very grateful to him. He was to keep me fed on delicious Nando's restaurant chicken meals for the next six days, and I will always feel deeply indebted to him for that kindness and generosity. The food in the cells was absolutely horrible.

Around two p.m. on Friday 23rd September I was taken to Rotten Row Magistrates' Court in Harare, but court proceedings for some reason kept being delayed. Around four p.m. the court proceedings finally commenced. The prosecutor told the court that I had been brought back from Canada following extradition proceedings that the State had instituted against me. The State would be opposing the granting of bail to me. In fact, I had not been extradited at all but had been deported from

Canada; extradition proceedings involved the issue and service of summons on me in Canada by Zimbabwe authorities, but no such summons had ever been served on me. Moreover, Zimbabwean authorities could not institute extradition proceedings against me while I was in Canada because there was no extradition agreement between Canada and Zimbabwe.

The prosecution was trying to mislead the court in an effort to justify my arrest; the prosecution now knew that the warrant of arrest that had been used to arrest me was invalid. Consequently, my arrest upon arrival in Zimbabwe could only have been lawful if it was pursuant to successful extradition proceedings. The prosecution was also aware that if my arrest had been unlawful because of an invalid warrant of arrest and the absence of extradition proceedings, then the issue of bail did not arise because I should not have been arrested in the first place.

Unfortunately, the junior lawyer who was representing me in court appeared to be struggling to understand the issues, and I realized that I needed a competent and experienced lawyer to handle my defense. I asked the junior lawyer to request the court to postpone the matter to the following Monday. I intended to make efforts over the weekend through my in-laws to get a competent and experienced lawyer to represent me.

The court postponed the matter to Monday 26th September 2011 but remanded me in custody. I was to be taken to Harare Remand Prison, a very notorious prison, to spend the weekend.

In a remand prison all the inmates are awaiting trial, and so ought to be presumed innocent until proven guilty in court. It made no sense to me why conditions in a remand prison are made very harsh, as if to punish inmates who are yet to be tried. I was to spend the six most difficult and painful days of my life in Harare Remand Prison beginning that Friday.

There have been two distinct occasions in my life when I really believed that my life was in imminent and grave danger. The first was in the year 1979 in Mozambique, during the Zimbabwe liberation war, when the military base I was staying in at Mavhonde in Manica Province came under intense military ground and air attack by Rhodesian security forces. Rhodesian soldiers often conducted military attacks on ZANLA bases in Mozambique, with the aim of crippling the capacity of the liberation fighters to conduct effective offensive attacks against the Rhodesian government inside Rhodesia. The attack at Mavhonde lasted almost a week and at one point during the attack I accidentally ran into a group of Rhodesian ground soldiers who had a clear view of me, and fled from them while they were shooting at me virtually at point blank range. I really could not believe that their bullets missed me. I thank God that I got away without even getting injured.

The second occasion was that Friday afternoon on 23rd September 2011, moments after I had been remanded in custody and was being transported to Harare Remand Prison. I was among a large number of prisoners who were put at the back of an enclosed, ten-tonne prison truck. We were so overcrowded in that truck that we were literally sitting on each other. I was handcuffed to another prisoner and the handcuffs felt tight and painful around the wrists. There were also at least five prison wardens guarding us. There was scarce ventilation at the back of that truck, in the form of tiny windows, which were very high up close to the roof on each side. It was a very hot late September afternoon and I prayed that we would quickly get to our destination and get out of that truck. September and October are two of the hottest months in Zimbabwe.

The truck drove from the Rotten Row Magistrates' Court in Harare into Rotten Row Road, going north, then passed the intersection with Samora Machel Avenue. It was meant to then turn right into Herbert Chitepo Avenue, but before making the right turn the truck's fuel ran out and it suddenly stopped. There was a lot of agitation and I realized from the verbal exchanges among the prison wardens that they needed to send someone to Chikurubi Maximum Security Prison to fetch diesel and come back to refuel the truck. My estimation was that this would take at least an hour.

I started to fear for my life. The prison wardens who had been sitting with us got out of the truck and shut the door behind them. They said they could not keep the door open because they feared that some prisoners might attempt to escape. It was so hot in that truck that I could hardly breathe. Some prisoners started to shout and pounded the steel walls of the truck from inside with their hands, demanding that the door be opened, but there was no response. It was becoming a riotous situation at the back of the truck and I feared an ugly scene was about to erupt. I was running out of breath and feared the worst.

After what seemed like hours, the prison truck got re-fuelled and then proceeded to Harare Remand Prison. We arrived in the early evening and I thanked God that I was alive.

Prisoners are accommodated in different and separate areas at Harare Remand Prison, according to the category that they fall under. There is a class C for minor offenders and juveniles, and a class D for offenders facing serious crimes. Class D offenders are those facing charges of murder, culpable homicide, robbery, rape and fraud; it is in this class that prisoners who are considered dangerous are kept. Since I was facing fraud charges I was kept in the class D area of the prison, together with those considered the most dangerous criminals. My clothes were taken away and I was made to wear a khaki uniform, which was so old and torn that it was in tatters.

We slept in a dormitory-like big cell which had an open toilet at one end. We were locked up in that cell, which was on the first floor of the building, at around four p.m. each day until the following morning. At around six in the morning we were taken out of the cell and would spend the day in a large courtyard on the ground floor, where we could take a cold shower and food would be served. The food was terrible and consisted of porridge in the morning and sadza (thick corn-meal porridge) with tripe or beans just before we got locked up for the night. There were prisoners who conducted church services during the day in the courtyard and there would be a lot of singing of gospel songs, which inspired some prisoners and gave them hope that one day they might get out of prison. Since this was a remand prison, all the prisoners were awaiting trial, and there was hope among many prisoners that they would be acquitted when they were tried in court.

Up in the dormitory cell there were storytellers, and we would listen to stories narrated by prisoners who felt they had experiences to share with other prisoners. This would go on for hours, until many of the prisoners fell asleep. There was a visiting hour on some days, but a prisoner had to be in handcuffs and leg-irons while meeting visitors. I wondered how those who came to visit me felt when they saw me in a torn khaki uniform, in handcuffs and leg-irons. It must have been a painful and shocking sight for them.

On Saturday 24th September 2011 I was in the court-yard during the day, when a number of prisoners came to me and told me that they had read in the newspapers about my deportation from Canada and my arrest upon arrival in Zimbabwe. Some people who visited prisoners brought with them not only food and drinks but also newspapers for their relatives or friends in prison to read. The prisoners who came to me felt that my arrest was politically motivated and they offered advice that they felt could be useful to me. One of them told me that he had been in trouble with the law often enough to know who were the best lawyers in town. He gave me a list of names of lawyers who he considered experienced and effective in handling criminal cases. The one lawyer who was very highly recommended by him and others was Advocate Nickiel Mushangwe, and I took note of the name and his contact details.

That Saturday afternoon I received a number of visitors during the visiting hour. Among them was my wife's cousin, who brought a delicious chicken meal, but I was to eat very little of it because the prisoners who had befriended me and offered me advice subtly expected repayment in the form of sharing with them the food that I received during visiting hours. My visitors also included my brother-in-law Gladman Chikwanda, who had driven all the way from Beitbridge on the Zimbabwe-South Africa border where he worked. I informed him and my wife's cousin that I desperately and urgently needed the services of a competent and experienced lawyer to handle my defense. I informed them that Advocate Mushangwe had been recommended to me and I requested them to urgently contact and ask him to come and meet me in prison, so that I could engage and brief him before my appearance in court on Monday 26th September 2011.

On Sunday 25th September 2011 a prison warden came and informed me that I had a visitor. He took me to an office in the prison compound, where a heavily-built man was seated in a chair. The man introduced himself to me as Nickiel Mushangwe, and I was enormously relieved to see him. I was very grateful to my brother- in-law and my wife's cousin for contacting the lawyer, and arranging for him to come to the prison to consult with me.

I briefed Advocate Mushangwe that Sunday morning in great detail. I told him that I had been deported from Canada but the prosecution was falsely claiming that I had been extradited, yet there was no extradition agreement between Zimbabwe and Canada. I explained that the warrant of arrest the police had acted upon to arrest me was invalid, because it was claimed in the warrant that it was issued as a result of my failure to appear in court for a remand hearing on 31st January 2000, yet I had in fact appeared in court on that date and the court had removed me from remand on that day.

Mr. Mushangwe quickly grasped the issues and explained that my arrest was unlawful in the circumstances. He added that since the arrest should not have been made and was unlawful, the question of bail did not even arise. He explained that there ought to be court records to confirm that I had appeared in court on 31st January 2000 and that the court had removed me from remand. He would go to the Clerk of Court early on Monday morning to obtain that court record and, once he had done so, it would be conclusive evidence that the warrant of arrest was invalid and that my arrest was unlawful. He was worried, however, that there was the risk that the court record may disappear if there were people in the

CIO and the police who were trying to conceal evidence and victimize me.

I was happy that Mr. Mushangwe was confident he would be able to get the court record before the court proceedings began on Monday. I advised him that a junior lawyer had represented me in court the previous Friday and that the issues involved had appeared to overwhelm him, so I had absolutely no confidence in him. Advocate Mushangwe assured me that he was taking over my legal representation and that he would do his best to convince the court that I had been unlawfully arrested by the police CID Fraud Squad. That Sunday night I slept well, even though the conditions were far from being comfortable or even humane in the remand prison. I had peace of mind because I was very hopeful. I was very grateful to my in-laws for contacting Advocate Mushangwe. They had shared the cost of my legal representation with my wife, whom they kept informed about everything that I was going through. My family was deeply worried back in Canada about the fact that I was in custody in Zimbabwe.

I was deeply relieved that Mr. Mushangwe had been available that weekend. Usually during weekends, lawyers and other professional people left town to spend the weekend resting in holiday resorts or in their country homes. I thanked God that Advocate Mushangwe had been in town that weekend, because it was critical that I met and briefed him that weekend in time for the court proceedings on Monday 26th September 2011.

Advocate Mushangwe spent the rest of that weekend investigating the circumstances surrounding the issuing of the warrant of arrest which had formed the basis of my arrest. He had extensive and very useful contacts in the police CID and the criminal justice system, and his investigations yielded the following information:

The police in Zimbabwe had been under immense pressure from the CIO to pursue me in Canada and to have me brought back to Zimbabwe, ever since my departure from Zimbabwe in the year 2001. While Chipanga and Mbalekwa were regularly making statements in Parliament claiming that I was a fugitive from justice and demanding that the Minister of Justice should take action to ensure that I was brought back from Canada, there was a parallel effort by the CIO, through the police, to push Canadian authorities to send me back to Zimbabwe. Maynard Muzariri in the CIO was working closely with the Zimbabwe police CID in this regard, and in the year 2008 there was email correspondence in which the CID formally requested Canadian immigration authorities to extradite me back to Zimbabwe, claiming that I was a fugitive from justice who was facing criminal charges in Zimbabwe. Following that request, Canadian authorities had requested to be furnished with documentary evidence by the Zimbabwe Republic Police of the nature of the charges that I was facing in Zimbabwe.

There was no such documentary evidence at that point. It was at that point that the CIO and the Zimbabwe Republic Police (ZRP) came up with the idea of a warrant of arrest to be used as the documentary evidence which had been requested by the Canadian authorities. Since up to the year 2008 there had been no such documentary evidence, in order to create such evidence a Chief Superintendent in the ZRP named Peter Magwenzi, in consultation with the CIO, then approached a senior magistrate and asked the magistrate to issue a warrant of arrest against me. A warrant was then issued against me in the year 2008, but the warrant was fraudulently made to look like it had been issued on 31st January 2000. The basis for the issuing of the warrant of arrest was the false claim that I had failed to appear in court for a remand hearing on 31st January 2000 and had instead absconded from Zimbabwe. Thus, for the warrant of arrest to be made to look genuine and valid, it was backdated to 31st January 2000. Here was a senior member of the judiciary, a senior magistrate, sitting down in the year 2008 with a senior police officer and deciding to issue a warrant of arrest dated 31st January 2000, in order to make it look like the warrant of arrest was being issued on 31st January 2000 because I had failed to appear in court on that day, yet this was in fact being done in 2008. Clearly the ZRP, CIO and a senior member of the judiciary were subverting the justice system in Zimbabwe and abusing their authority to victimize me. If ever evidence was needed to show that the judiciary in Zimbabwe had been captured by the executive to serve political interests, and that the judiciary received orders from the executive, this was it.

The warrant of arrest was then taken by the ZRP and sent to Interpol, in support of a request that there should be an international effort to arrest me. In particular, Interpol was requested to approach Canadian authorities and present the warrant of arrest to them with a view to commencing extradition proceedings against me. The international police organization Interpol was at that time being headed by none other than Augustine Chihuri, the then Zimbabwean Police Commissioner General. How a credible organization like Interpol could elect a Police Commissioner General from a regime the international community considers rogue to head the organization is mind-boggling, but it is clear that Zimbabwe abused its leadership of Interpol by using a forged warrant of arrest to persuade the Canadian government through Interpol to send me back to Zimbabwe.

However, this attempt at extraditing me soon ran into the difficulty that there was no extradition agreement between Zimbabwe and Canada. The effort to extradite me was consequently abandoned, but Zimbabwe authorities continued to put pressure on Canadian authorities to send me back to Zimbabwe.

There being no extradition agreement between Canada and Zimbabwe, but willing to accede to the request by Zimbabwean authorities to send me back to Zimbabwe, Canadian authorities decided to use the deportation procedure to achieve the same result that an extradition process would have achieved had it been competent: namely my removal from Canada and enforced return to Zimbabwe.

Advocate Mushangwe was struck by the irony of it all. Canadian authorities had claimed that they were deporting me because I had served the Mugabe regime in a senior role, and because they were highly critical of that regime they objected to my stay in Canada, since I was associated with the Mugabe regime. Yet here were Canadian authorities working closely with those same rogue Zimbabwean authorities, but trying to conceal the fact by adopting the deportation procedure. The deportation procedure gave the appearance of Canadian authorities acting independently in sending me back to Zimbabwe, without being prompted to do so by Zimbabwean authorities, yet in reality they were subtly complying with Zimbabwe's request to send me back to Zimbabwe. If the Canadian authorities had really detested the Mugabe regime they should not have cooperated with it nor acceded to the request by the Zimbabwe authorities to send me back to Zimbabwe. Moreover, if the Mugabe regime was as brutal as claimed by the Canadian authorities, then my enforced return to Zimbabwe would put my life in danger and the Canadian authorities would be complicit in my persecution by the Zimbabwe authorities.

In addition to establishing all these facts, Advocate Mushangwe also went to the Clerk of Court at the Magistrates' Court on Monday 26th September 2011, and he obtained the actual court record of the proceedings that had taken place on 31st January 2000. The record conclusively showed that I had not only appeared in court, but also that the court had removed me and my co-accused from remand and set us free on 31st January 2000.

In court that Monday morning, on 26th September 2011, the prosecution claimed that I had been extradited from Canada and that I had been arrested lawfully. Consequently, the prosecution was objecting to the granting of bail. On the other hand, Advocate Mushangwe presented all the facts very elaborately to the presiding magistrate and produced the court record of 31st January 2000 as an exhibit. He explained that the warrant of arrest was not only invalid but that it had been issued irregularly and with malice at the request of the ZRP and the CIO, and was therefore unlawful. In the circumstances, he argued, the issue of bail did not arise because I should not have been arrested in the first place.

The magistrate reserved judgment and adjourned the matter to the following day. I was sent back to Harare Remand Prison where I spent another night in inhumane conditions. The following morning, Tuesday 27th September, I met Advocate Mushangwe before the court proceedings resumed and he told me that the magistrate was under immense pressure from the ZRP and CIO to rule against me in the matter. He indicated that the magistrate was starting to fear for his life. Advocate Mushangwe, however, remained confident that the magistrate would rule in my favour because the court record was conclusive evidence that the warrant of arrest was invalid and had been issued unlawfully.

The presiding magistrate adjourned the matter again that Tuesday morning to the following day. I spent another day and night in Harare Remand Prison until the following morning, when judgment was finally handed down. In a judgement on Wednesday 28th September 2011 in the matter "The State v Lovemore Itai Mukandi", case number 6527/11, the magistrate handed down the following judgement:

"After hearing submissions by both counsels, the court finds the following:

"It is common cause that this is the same case which was refused remand on 31/01/00. It is also common cause that there is no extradition treaty between Zimbabwe and Canada. The court finds that the accused person is before the court as a result of his deportation from Canada and not extradition... The legal issue to be resolved is whether or not the issue of bail arises in this case. From the documentary exhibits filed of record, it is clear that the accused person did not abscond trial or breach any bail condition... What we have is a warrant of arrest issued on 31/01/00. The (court record) shows that this is the same date when further remand of the accused person was refused. It therefore follows that his warrant of arrest which the State is acting on was obtained erroneously, since it does not tell the truth about the records... Thus the issue of bail does not arise, since the accused person did not abscond trial as alleged. Wherefore, the warrant of arrest issued on 31/01/00 is hereby cancelled..."

Thus I was set free by the court on Wednesday 28th September 2011. I had been under custody of the Canada Border Services Agency from three a.m. on Wednesday 21st September 2011, until I arrived at Robert Gabriel Mugabe International Airport in Harare. I had been arrested on arrival at the Robert Gabriel Mugabe Airport on Thursday 22nd September 2011. I had spent the night of 22nd September 2011 in police cells at Harare Central Police Station and on 23rd September 2011 I had been taken to Harare Remand Prison, where I was kept in prison cells until 28th September 2011. Up to this day, as I write this autobiography I cannot enter Canada to be reunited with my family, because Canadian authorities will not allow me to re-enter after my deportation. All of this because of a warrant of arrest which was fraudulently and unlawfully issued against me at the request of the Zimbabwe Republic Police working in concert with the CIO, who were after me just because I did not share and still do not share their wish that Zimbabwe should be ruled by Mnangagwa.

I will state here that I have always been very apprehensive about the prospect of Mnangagwa being President of Zimbabwe. I have known him from personal experience over the years to be highly tribalistic and to have an exclusive rather than an inclusive approach in politics. His political outlook sees Masvingo/Midlands provinces as being synonymous with Zimbabwe and is not national in character. He is corrupt and cruel and does not have the qualities of a national leader. Mnangagwa is far from being presidential.

I thought President Mugabe had correctly seen leadership qualities in Dr. Sydney Sekeramayi, but was worried about his timid nature. Over the years that I worked closely with him, I thought Dr. Sekeramayi was highly humane and inclusive in his approach. He had the backing of General Mujuru who, though corrupt, was also very humane and inclusive in nature. General Mujuru and Dr. Sekeramayi never displayed any tribalistic tendencies. I have no doubt that Zimbabwe would have done very well under Dr. Sekeramayi or someone with the same political outlook and humane nature as him.

Mugabe made the mistake of clinging to power for too long, oblivious of the fact that Mnangagwa used that time to consolidate his plot to unseat him, until it was too late for Mugabe to implement his succession plan. Mugabe's hold on the levers of State power had been neutralized by Mnangagwa by then.

Even though I was set free by the court around ten in the morning of Wednesday 28th September 2011, prison authorities told me there was no transport that could immediately take me back to Harare Remand Prison for my release from prison to be processed. I was made to spend the whole day in cells in the basement of the court building. It was not until after five p.m. that day that I was taken back, together with other prisoners to Harare Remand Prison. The process of my release took a few more hours and I only walked out of Harare Remand Prison around ten p.m. on Wednesday 28th September 2011.

My wife's cousin picked me up from the prison gate, and he had a big and most pleasant surprise for me: he had booked me into the Cresta Lodge Hotel in Msasa, Harare for the night. I badly needed such a facility. My hair and clothes had lice all over, and I needed to fill a bathtub with very hot water and soak my hair in that hot water to kill them. I did that and then took a very hot bath until I felt I had got rid of the lice from other hairy areas of my body. I then soaked all my clothes in near-boiling water for the night. My wife's cousin may never know what a blessing he was to me during the most difficult period of my life, but I will always be grateful to him for that. I am also very grateful to Gladman Chikwanda for facilitating my legal representation through Advocate Mushangwe.

My persecution by the police and the CIO did not end there. The police and CIO continued to put pressure on the criminal justice system to victimize me. To that end, while I was waiting to be released from the Harare Remand Prison on 28th September 2011, I was served a summons by the Police to appear in the magistrates' court on 15th December 2011 for trial on the original fraud charges.

I appeared in court on 15th December 2011, but the prosecutor told the court that the Police had misplaced the docket and the record could not be found. The matter was postponed to 9th January 2012 and was then again postponed to 17th January 2012, because the State was still not ready to commence trial. My lawyers were convinced that the prosecution felt uncomfortable proceeding to trial because they did not have any evidence against me, but they were under immense pressure from the Police and CIO to be seen to be making an effort to pursue the matter.

Meanwhile Advocate Julia Wood, who was representing my co- accused alongside Advocate Wilson Manase, had taken over from Advocate Mushangwe as my defense lawyer, and on 17th January 2012 she and Manase made an application in the magistrates' court to have the criminal matter referred to the Supreme Court, to determine whether my constitutional rights and those of my co-accused had not been infringed by the prolonged delay in proceeding to trial, because we had originally been arrested in March 1999 and it was now thirteen years since that initial arrest. I was examined and cross-examined at length in court, to determine the nature and extent of the delays by the prosecution to commence trial, and on 1st February 2012 the presiding magistrate granted the application to refer the matter to the Supreme Court, expressing the view that the delay in this case to commence trial was grossly unreasonable. This was an application for a permanent stay of prosecution and was to be heard by the Constitutional Court, which was created in terms of a national referendum held in Zimbabwe in the year 2013.

Meanwhile, Advocate Wood prepared legal papers on my behalf to institute civil proceedings against the State, arising from my unlawful arrest and detention at Harare

Central Police Station and Harare Remand Prison during the period 22nd September 2011 to 28th September 2011 inclusive, as well as my arrest all the way from Canada to Harare airport, while I was under guard by the two officers from the Canada Border Services Agency. The civil claim also arose from the defamation I suffered from the false claim by the Zimbabwe police in the media in Zimbabwe, and to Interpol and Canadian authorities, that I was a fugitive from justice who had fled from Zimbabwe in the year 2001. Advocate Wood served notice to sue the State in March 2012 under the State Liabilities Act, and then issued summons on my behalf against the State in May 2012. My civil claim for U.S.$10 million damages against the State is pending in the Zimbabwe High Court under file number HC 5434/12. The matter was not pursued by my lawyers after they grew cold feet. I made inquiries in 2020 about the status of the civil claim but was advised informally by an official in the Ministry of Justice that the file containing my civil claim was sent to the National Archives on the orders of the Mnangagwa post-coup administration. I believe that one day there will be a law-abiding government in Zimbabwe which will be willing to settle this matter.

Sometime in the year 2014 the Constitutional Court in Harare heard my application for a permanent stay of prosecution, but dismissed it and ruled that I and my co-accused could still be tried on the original fraud charges, notwithstanding the long time that had lapsed since our initial arrest. I believe that judgment is another testimony of the capture of the Zimbabwe judiciary at the highest level by the executive arm of the State. My lawyers got to know of that judgement weeks before it was delivered from other lawyers, who overheard informal discussions some of the judges were having with members of the police and CIO, who were influencing them to come up with that judgement. However, due to the passage of time, the witnesses the prosecution had intended to call and some of my co-accused were either deceased or had left the country permanently by 2014, and it was just not feasible for the prosecution to proceed with the trial. It was like nature finally put to an end the ordeal that I had endured for close to twenty years at the hands of the Zimbabwe police and the CIO.

It is important to note that the debate of who would succeed President Mugabe was still raging in the year 2014, and my persecution by the police and the CIO continued to be motivated by this succession battle.

IN THE YEAR 2014 my application was accepted by the University of Cape Town (U.C.T.) in South Africa, to study on a full-time basis for a PhD degree in Economics. The PhD program comprised intensive coursework and a dissertation. I left Zimbabwe on 31st December 2014 for Cape Town, and I began my studies in January 2015; by December 2017 I had completed the coursework.

I started working on the dissertation in January 2018. The dissertation is in the area of macroeconomics and monetary policy in particular, and the title is: "Essays on Central Bank Independence, Monetary Policy Transmission Mechanisms and Financial Stability in Canada". I selected Canada for my model because I did my undergraduate and master's level studies in Economics in Canada, and I am therefore familiar with the Canadian databases and other research tools. I used vector auto-regression (V.A.R.) analysis for the model. At the time of writing this autobiography in February/March 2020, I had handed in a draft of the dissertation to my supervisor Professor Haim Abraham, as the first stage of having the dissertation assessed by examiners. I still have to formally submit a final draft to the examiners.

My life on the whole has not been an easy one. I was subjected to persecution by Zimbabwean authorities for decades, for political reasons as described above. I have also had the rare and hurtful experience of having parents and some close relatives who have sought to pull me down and destroy me. My mother in particular sat in a dark place, and was very divisive in the family. She also actively encouraged the efforts by my ex-wife to turn my children against me.

I sacrificed a lot of financial resources and effort to educate the children I have with my ex-wife. They went to the best schools in Zimbabwe; Bryan went to St John's Preparatory School in Borrowdale in Harare for his primary school, and to Peterhouse near Marondera for his secondary and high school education. He went to the University of Zimbabwe and became a qualified medical doctor after that. His sister Tamara went to the Dominican Convent in Harare for her primary and high school education, while Tamara's younger sister Tanaka went to Borrowdale Primary School. They have all done very well in life; Bryan lives in Australia while Tamara and Tanaka are now Canadian citizens working in financial institutions in Toronto. However, their mother, who did not show much interest in their education as they grew up, suddenly became close to them as they completed their studies and has turned all three of them against me – indeed, so much that I only got to learn of the marriage and wedding of Tamara and Tanaka through the grapevine and from social media. None of the three children I had with my ex-wife communicate with me, because of the negative influence of my ex-wife, with the encouragement of some of my close relatives.

My ex-wife turned my children against me because she thought that if we remained close they would extend financial assistance to me, which would filter through to my wife Sibongile and our daughters Lisa and Kundisai, and she was opposed to that. However, it turns out that God has blessed us and Lisa is now working in risk assessment and management for a leading Canadian bank in Toronto, after graduating from the University of Toronto. Kundisai graduated from the University of Toronto and is working in Toronto.

My wife Sibongile has defied all the odds over the years and has provided for every need for the family. She has worked for a leading Canadian telecommunications company since the year 2005 and has pursued private studies on a part-time basis, until she qualified as a Chartered Professional Accountant (CPA) of Canada. I will forever be grateful to Sibongile for her resilience and for the role that she has so successfully played of being the mother and man of the house, in my absence over the years. I thank God for guiding her, and for protecting me and my family from the evil forces which have demonstrated over the years a determination to destroy us.

ABOUT THE AUTHOR

Lovemore Mukandi is a legal practitioner registered with the High Court of Zimbabwe, an economist and an author.

He holds BL and LLB degrees from the University of Zimbabwe; BA Hons Economics and B Commerce (major in Finance) from Saint Mary's University in Halifax, as well as MA in Economics from Carleton University in Ottawa, Canada. He is working on submitting his PhD dissertation in Economics (on Monetary Policy and Central Bank Independence) to the University of Cape Town, South Africa.

Lovemore participated in the Zimbabwe war of liberation in Mozambique, during the years 1978-80. After Zimbabwe's independence, he worked as a diplomat in the Zimbabwe embassy in Mozambique, and in Romania during the years 1980-83, then resumed his law studies at the University of Zimbabwe in 1984, graduating in 1986.

He worked in the Central Intelligence Organization (CIO) after graduation and was legal advisor and assistant to the Minister of State for National Security in the President's Office during the period 1988-93. He was then appointed Director of Administration in the CIO. In 1998, President Mugabe appointed him Deputy Director General of the CIO.

Lovemore is expecting the publication soon of his second book, an academic book: *A Handbook on the Basics of Matrices and Matrix Algebra Operations.*

Lovemore is married to Sibongile, a Chartered Professional Accountant and Author, and they have two daughters. He has two daughters and a son from an earlier marriage.

www.ingramcontent.com/pod-product-compliance
Lightning Source LLC
Chambersburg PA
CBHW051832130726
47987CB00002B/516